BECAUSE
OF THE
CHRIST
ON
CALVARY

BECAUSE
OF THE
CHRIST
ON
CALVARY

BRAD WILCOX

**DESERET
BOOK**

SALT LAKE CITY, UTAH

To my friend Russ Greiner,
who joined the Church at Brigham Young University,
served his mission in Wyoming and Montana,
and has tirelessly taught about Christ
and His gospel ever since.

© 2020 The Brad and Debi Wilcox Family Trust

Visit us at deseretbook.com

Library of Congress Cataloging-in-Publication Data
CIP data on file
ISBN 978-1-62972-748-6

Printed in the United States of America
PubLitho, Draper, UT

10   9   8   7   6   5   4   3   2   1

CONTENTS

EASTER'S PROOFS
CHRIST'S WITNESSES PAST AND PRESENT

EASTER'S PROMISES
THE BLESSINGS OF WORSHIP AND DISCIPLESHIP

ACKNOWLEDGMENTS

When George Durrant was asked why he wrote books, he answered, "I am just a better person when I have a book hatching." I have found the same to be true for me. Writing helps me live and worship more consciously. I am indebted to many who help in my book-hatching process. Thanks to my wife, Debi, and our family for their patience, support, and love. I especially appreciate my son David and good friend Brett Sanders for taking time to review the manuscript despite their busy schedules. Thanks to Cody Sanders, who helps keep me going.

I appreciate Sai Maddali, Crystal Anderson, Jenny Reeder, Ryan and Silvia London, and Evan Wilkinson for allowing me to share their amazing stories. Thanks to President Jeremy and Sister Jenny Guthrie of the Texas Houston South Mission, who told me about Evan Wilkinson, and to President David and Sister Deb Checketts of the England London Mission, whose purpose statement for their missionaries gave me the organizational structure I needed for this book. Thanks also to Lisa Roper at Deseret Book for being my wonderful product director, advocate, and friend. I also appreciate Tracy Keck, Shauna Gibby, Breanna Anderl, Kenny Hodges, Guy Randall, and the rest of the Deseret Book team. In addition, hats off to Erin Hallstrom, KaRyn Lay, Danielle Wagner, Jasmine Mullen, and Colin Rivera for all the good they do at *LDS Living*.

Finally, thanks to longtime friends and colleagues at Brigham Young University: Timothy G. Morrison, Camille Fronk Olson, Brent L. Top, Sandra Rogers, JD Hucks, and Bruce Payne. They have all influenced countless lives— including mine.

INTRODUCTION

I have celebrated the Holy Week and Easter in Africa as a child, in South America as a missionary, and in Europe when my wife and I directed a study abroad program there for Brigham Young University. I remember smelling incense in the Coptic Christian churches in Ethiopia and watching processions in Chilean streets in which people carried platforms on their shoulders holding statues covered with flowers. I recall people carrying palm leaves on the streets of Spain in preparation for Palm Sunday. I love the fact that so many people worldwide remember Christ's suffering, death, and Resurrection. Still, many others do not know or care.

My wife and I exited a subway station in a large and crowded city. We saw representatives from a church standing near a nice display of their religious literature. I greeted them, but no one else even glanced in their direction. A few blocks later, we encountered a man waving a sign that said, "Hell is real. Don't go there. Accept Jesus now!" I smiled at the man, but everyone else ignored him. Our missionaries often get the same treatment. It is almost laughable to see the lengths to which some people go to avoid talking with a person wearing a plaque. People appear to have no interest in God, Jesus, or religion. Nevertheless, they all desire a better life.

As sure as an inborn moral compass, there is an upward reach within us. Deep inside, people want something better for themselves and those they love. Immigrants and refugees move across the globe, and parents seek better jobs for themselves and better education for their children. People search for health and happiness. The problem is that they blow off anyone who proposes that God and religion are a means to reaching their goals. They want a better life, but not God. They want happiness, but not religion. They have yet to connect the dots and realize that the only one who can truly satisfy their upward reaching is the King on the cross, the Christ on Calvary.

Christ is a title as well as a name. It is the Greek translation of the Hebrew word *Messiah* and means "Anointed One" (see Bible Dictionary, "Christ"). *Calvary* is the place where our Lord was crucified. It is the Latin translation of the Hebrew word *Golgotha*, meaning "a skull" or "place of the skull" (Bible Dictionary, 611). Taken together, the words mean Christ was anointed to suffer and die for us, and by choosing to do so, He brought hope to everyone who has ever longed to do and be better.

At the beginning of His ministry, Jesus stood in the synagogue in Nazareth and read from Isaiah: "The Spirit of the Lord God is upon me; because the Lord hath anointed me to preach good tidings" (61:1). Surely, His listeners had heard others read the scripture before, but now Jesus added, "This day is this scripture fulfilled in your ears" (Luke 4:21). In other words, "I am the source of the abundant life you seek. I am the Anointed One of whom I just read. I have power to heal and help you. I am the Messiah, the Christ." The people accused Him of blasphemy and tried to kill Him, but that did not change the truth of His words. Latter-day Saints testify that in the premortal existence Jesus became "the one anointed of the Father to be His personal representative in all things pertaining to the salvation of mankind" (Bible Dictionary, 592–93). To that end, He died for us on Calvary (see Luke 23:33).

Our covenant relationship with Christ allows for a fullness of hope! That hope is the message of Easter, and in a world that is increasingly apathetic about God and religion, Easter matters more than ever. People can call it spring break if they want, but Easter will eternally be

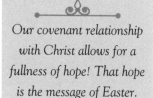

Our covenant relationship with Christ allows for a fullness of hope! That hope is the message of Easter.

about the Christ on Calvary. "It is the day that changed everything."[1] In this book, I invite you to consider what you really want most and then connect the dots: It is only as you believe in God and have faith in Christ that you "might with surety hope for a better world" (Ether 12:4). "Seek ye first the kingdom of God, and his righteousness," taught the Savior, "and all [else] . . . shall be added unto you" (Matthew 6:33).

Let us deepen our appreciation of the Savior and His grace. Let us peel back the layers of His Atonement and reflect on how it applies to us personally. Let us consider the witnesses of Christ's reality, past and present, and stand in reverent awe at how that reality can change our worship and discipleship—how it can ultimately change us.

Because of the Christ on Calvary, we can know that the Creation, the Fall, and His Atonement are all part of an eternal plan for our progress and joy. Not only can we find answers to the questions of human suffering but also the help Jesus offers in the midst of the suffering. Because of the Christ on Calvary, we understand that no matter how many people give up on God, He never gives up on us. We can hold on to faith and receive the divine assistance we need to repent and become better. Because of Christ, spirituality and religion matter. Worship and discipleship matter. Truth matters. We matter—all because of the Christ on Calvary.

EASTER'S PURPOSES

The Savior and His Grace

Ask any Christian child why we celebrate Easter and you will hear the word *Jesus*. It may be mixed in with Easter baskets and candy, but Jesus will be there. What these children—and some adults—have yet to learn is *why* we needed Jesus in first place. In this section, let us examine the Fall and the far-reaching effects of Christ's infinite Atonement. Let us retrace the Savior's activities during the final week before His Resurrection—including His suffering and death on the cross—and better understand scriptures that reveal the purposes of Easter.

CHRIST AT THE CROSSROADS

We do not know exactly where Christ was hung on the cross, but Romans typically performed crucifixions along busy roadways. They wanted everyone to see the suffering victims so people would get—and spread—the message that Rome would not tolerate any rebellion. Whether Christ was crucified west or north of Jerusalem, it was surely at a crossroads.

Similarly, we do not know exactly where Saul had his vision. He was journeying to Damascus to search for followers of Christ and "bring them bound unto Jerusalem" (Acts 9:2). Damascus was a cultural and commercial center that connected the lands of the Mediterranean with the Orient. Jewish leaders feared that if Christianity got a foothold there, it would spread across the world. Saul's vision came at a crossroads.

God sent Christ in the meridian of time—the central point of mortal history.[1] Every prophet before then looked forward to Christ's Atonement through sacrifices. Every prophet since then looked back to His Atonement through the sacrament. God did not send Christ to threaten or stop anyone, but to save everyone. For this purpose, Christ was sent at a crossroads.

The crossroads I have described here are points at which roads intersect or pivotal moments in time. However, the term can also describe critical decisions: Am I going to choose to believe Christ or doubt Him, accept Him or reject Him, love Him or ignore Him? In order to make such choices, we must understand why Christ came in the first place, and that brings us to the Creation and the Fall.

God is a creator, but He did not create our eternal essences. We coexisted with God (see D&C 93:22–23, 29). Joseph Smith taught that God offered us the "privilege to advance like himself . . . [and] be exalted with himself."[2] He and Heavenly Mother clothed us with spirit bodies just as earthly parents clothed our spirits with physical bodies. Elder Tad R. Callister said, "There is a sentiment among many in the world that we are the spirit creations of God, just as a building is the creation of its architect or a painting the creation of its painter. . . . [Yet] can a mere creation ever become like its creator? Can a building ever become an architect? A painting a painter?"[3] No, but we can become like God because our spirits were "begotten and born," as President Joseph F. Smith taught, "of heavenly parents."[4]

After our spirits' births, we progressed in our premortal existence until we could learn no more without a mortal school. That is why God needed to initiate and oversee the Creation of the world. We do not know everything about *how* the earth was created, but we know *why*. God created it for the education and progress of His children.

My daughter Whitney once went camping with some friends in the beautiful canyons of southern Utah. As the group hiked amid the dramatic rock formations, they talked about how long it must have taken water to work away at the stones to shape the landscape they saw. At night, Whitney and her friends stared up at the star-filled sky. Instead of being filled with reverent awe, one girl said, "Seeing such numerous creations makes me feel so small and insig-

> *We do not know everything about* how *the earth was created, but we know* why.

nificant. I don't think God knows me or cares about my life."

Whitney said, "It has the opposite effect on me. It reminds me that God created all of this for us so we could grow, gain experiences, and have joy."[5] Indeed, God's creations do not need to stand as evidence of His distance from us, but can instead witness of His ability to be close to us. Surely a God who possesses the knowledge and power to create the world also has whatever it takes to be able to love and care for each child who inhabits it.

Elder Dieter F. Uchtdorf said, "While we may look at the vast expanse of the universe and say, 'What is man in comparison to the glory of creation?' God Himself said we are the reason He created the universe! His work and glory—the purpose for this magnificent universe—is to save and exalt mankind [see Moses 1:38–39]."[6]

Along with the Creation, the Fall was also necessary for our progress. If Adam and Eve had stayed in the garden, they would have been like Peter Pan, refusing to grow up. I once saw a young man wearing a T-shirt that said, "Don't grow up. It's a trap!" I laughed, but I have to disagree. Growing up is not a trap. It is the goal.

For centuries, Christians have blamed Adam and Eve for messing up what could have been a pretty easy existence, but Latter-day Saints honor them for realizing there had to be more to life than merely existing. Latter-day Saint educator Randall C. Bird wrote, "Had they been forced out of the garden, or placed in a fallen world to begin with, they would have been inclined to blame God for all their challenges, sorrows, and sins."[7] Whether or not there was another way for Adam and Eve to enter mortality, they ended up right where God wanted them to be. The difficulty of this earthly school may be why a third of our spirit siblings refused to come, but the possibility of growth associated with it is what made the rest of us jump at the chance.

Some wonder why God gave Adam and Eve seemingly

conflicting commandments by telling them to have children but not to partake of the fruit of the tree of knowledge of good and evil. Perhaps God was teaching Adam and Eve—and through them, all of us—how to use agency thoughtfully and make moral judgments. Heavenly Father knew that Adam and Eve were entering a world where not every choice would be clear-cut and where they would often have to select the best of several good options. Adam and Eve's choice brought death and sin into the world, but it also brought us and Jesus into the world. That made it the best choice. Eve said, "Were it not for our transgression we never should have had seed, and never should have known good and evil, and the joy of our redemption, and the eternal life which God giveth unto all the obedient" (Moses 5:11).

Once Adam and Eve had partaken of the fruit of the tree of knowledge of good and evil, God guarded the tree of life (see Alma 42:2). The fruit of that tree would have been fine for Adam and Eve to eat when they were immortal, but it became forbidden once they fell because if they had eaten it at that point, they would have been immortal in their sins with no hope of ever becoming celestial. Immortal is not the same as mature. In the garden, Adam and Eve could repent, but they could not be refined. They could be forgiven, but not perfected.[8] They needed to grow up. They needed to Fall and enter mortality. They needed Christ's Atonement.

Some wonder why Satan tempted Adam and Eve. After

all, if Satan had really wanted to mess up God's plan, he could have simply left them in the garden. We are told Satan did not know the mind of God (see Moses 4:6), but he surely knew the plan of salvation. He was in the pre-mortal existence and had no veil placed over his memory. Satan certainly could have messed up God's plan by refusing to tempt Adam and Eve, but that would have messed up *his* plan. He knew he could not win in the end, so his only motivation was to hurt God as deeply as he could by pulling away more of His children (see 2 Nephi 2:27). The sooner Adam and Eve had posterity, the sooner Satan could do damage. The minute there were souls to steal, Satan's work could proceed, but fortunately, the minute there were souls to save, God's work could proceed as well. Christ came to save us from the physical and spiritual deaths that came in consequence of the Fall (see 2 Nephi 9:10). In addition, He saved us from a fate worse than either: life without purpose, learning, growth, and progress.

Christ was there at the crossroads of the Creation and the Fall so we could choose to progress. Christ's Atonement came at the crossroads of history so we could choose to progress, but none of that matters until we meet Him at another crossroads—the crossroads of our individual lives.

I first met Sai when he attended one of my lectures at Brigham Young University Education Week. He told me he was a convert of less than a year and would soon be attending school there. I promised to keep in touch with him.

Sai's parents had moved to the United States from India and settled in Georgia, where they reared their son as a Hindu. Sai graduated from high school and received a scholarship to Georgia State University in Atlanta. At freshman orientation, he met a Latter-day Saint girl, Sariah, and they became friends. She invited him to church, where he met the sister missionaries and agreed to listen to their lessons. They told him he was a child of God—something he had never heard before. They said, "We lived as spirit children of our Father in Heaven before we were born on this earth. We were not, however, like our Heavenly Father, nor could we ever become like Him and enjoy all the blessings that He enjoys without the experience of living in mortality with a physical body. God's whole purpose . . . is to enable each of us to enjoy all His blessings" (*Preach My Gospel*, 48). Sai said to me later, "Their words gave me a great feeling of comfort."

Christ's Atonement came at the crossroads of history so we could choose to progress, but none of that matters until we meet Him at another crossroads—the crossroads of our individual lives.

Sai kept attending church and began reading the Book of Mormon. Whenever the sisters talked about baptism, he responded, "I enjoy learning about your religion, but I don't want to join." They scheduled the next lesson at the Atlanta temple grounds, where they taught how families can be together forever. Sai recalled, "As someone who had lived his whole life away from most of his extended family, I felt a longing to have what the sisters described."

Sai continued reading and praying, but he did not think he could get baptized without receiving some grand and dramatic manifestation from God. Then he thought of how God had already manifested Himself. Weren't new friends, answers to questions, and peaceful feelings manifestations from God? Didn't so many ordinary blessings add up to something extraordinary?

One day while on a walk with Sariah, he surprised her by blurting out, "I want to be baptized." They called the sisters and told them the news. Back at his dorm, Sai called his parents and said, "I have chosen to become a follower of Jesus Christ." His father and mother felt like their son was turning his back on them and his heritage.

It was a crossroads for Sai. He stood between his Hindu past and a Christian future. He asked himself, "Am I just doing this for Sariah and her family? Is it just because I live in a place where Christians are a majority and I want to fit in?" No. He knew his choice to be baptized was not because Sariah and the missionaries had come into his life, but because Christ had come into his life. He proceeded.

After the baptismal service, his bishop, Bishop Colton, said, "Sai, I know this was hard for you. I am proud of you. As you were being baptized, I felt such a strong presence. I know your ancestors were watching you with happiness. They are proud of you too." Sai had not expected to hear that message, but he needed it. Deep down, he still wondered if joining the Church made him less Indian and if he were forsaking his cultural heritage. Bishop Colton's testimony helped confirm the correctness of his decision.

The next day in church, Sai was confirmed and received the gift of the Holy Ghost. He felt the love of everyone in the congregation as well as the love of God and Christ. He knew he was not alone.

Because of the Christ on Calvary, the Creation and the Fall have purpose. Because of the Christ on Calvary, each person can choose to progress. Christ meets each of us at our crossroads and beckons, "Come unto me" (Matthew 11:28). Many refuse, so imagine the Savior's joy when some, like Sai, say, "I will." The world once measured years in relation to coming before or after Christ. Now it is politically correct to speak of before and after a common era. That does not change the fact that Sai and all of us must ultimately measure the years of our lives as coming before or after the crossroads at which we meet the Christ on Calvary.

AN INFINITE
AND ETERNAL SACRIFICE

When Debi and I were on our mission in Chile, we loved going out with the missionaries. One day when Debi was with two elders, a man approached them in the street and asked, "Are you Christians?"

Debi said, "We most certainly are."

The man then surprised her by saying, "Well, I'm not."

"Why not?" asked one of the elders.

"Because Jesus was a Jew. If I have to have a Savior, I want Him to be Chilean."

When Debi got home and related the experience, I chuckled at this man's strong sense of patriotism. Yet, his statement got us thinking. Why was Christ born a Jew in the Middle East? Why couldn't He have been born in South America, Asia, Africa, or anywhere else?

Debi finally found an answer in 2 Nephi 10:3: "It must needs be expedient that Christ . . . should come among the Jews, among those who are the more wicked part of the world; and they shall crucify him . . . , and there is none other nation on earth that would crucify their God." Harsh, but before we become too critical of the ancient Jews, let us remember what President Brigham Young said about the rest of us: "I suppose that God never organized an earth and peopled it that was ever reduced to a lower state of darkness, sin and ignorance than ours. I suppose this is one of the lowest kingdoms that ever the Lord Almighty created."[1] Christ came to the lowest nation in one of the lowest worlds. Truly, He descended below all things.

Nephites and Lamanites had to know about the Jews because of their heritage and because Jesus would live among them. The Jews never knew about the inhabitants of ancient America. Similarly, there are children of God on other worlds who know about us, although we do not know about them. They must learn about our world because this is where Christ performed the Atonement, which also covers them. The fact that Christ's Atonement extends to worlds beyond our own is one of the reasons it is called "infinite" (2 Nephi 9:7), but there are others.

Amulek taught, "For it is expedient that there should be a great and last sacrifice; yea, not a sacrifice of man, neither of beast, neither of any manner of fowl; for it shall not be a human sacrifice; but it must be an infinite and eternal sacrifice. . . . And that great and last sacrifice will be the Son of God, yea, infinite and eternal" (Alma 34:10, 14).

We typically think of the word *infinite* as meaning without end. However, Christ's Atonement does not cover every world ever created or every world yet to be created. President Russell M. Nelson taught that Christ's Atonement extends to all the "worlds created by Him."[2] Thus, Amulek's words "infinite and eternal" do not only describe Christ's sacrifice, but Christ Himself—"the Son of God, [who is] infinite and eternal" (Alma 34:14). In the Doctrine and Covenants, we learn that the word *endless* describes God (see D&C 19:4, 10): "Endless punishment is God's punishment" (v. 12). In the same way, the words *infinite Atonement* can describe Christ's Atonement.

Jesus, the firstborn of all God's spirit children, was the only one qualified, capable, and authorized to be the Christ. Elder James E. Talmage wrote, "For the great sacrifice, the effects of which were to be infinite, only an innocent subject could be accepted. It was Christ's right to become the Savior as the only sinless being on earth, and the Only Begotten of the Father, and above all as the one ordained in the heavens to be the Redeemer of mankind."[3] Truly, there is "no other name" through which we can be saved (Mosiah 3:17; see also Moses 6:52; D&C 18:23; Acts 4:12).

> *Jesus, the firstborn of all God's spirit children, was the only one qualified, capable, and authorized to be the Christ.*

Nevertheless, people continue to look elsewhere (see Jacob 4:14). Some people leave the Church because they feel like too much is expected of them. They may attend other Christian churches for a while, but often leave those as well because it seems intolerant to believe that all people have to accept Jesus. Finally, they settle on believing in a higher power. No callings. No commandments. No intolerance. The only problem is that there is no happiness or peace either, not really. Christian author C. S. Lewis wrote, "God cannot give us a happiness and peace apart from Himself, because it is not there. There is no such thing."[4] These people discover their "higher power" asks nothing, but offers nothing.[5] In contrast, Heavenly Father asks much, but offers everything.

The Savior taught, "For wide is the gate, and broad is the way, that leadeth to destruction, and many there be which go in thereat. . . . Strait is the gate, and narrow is the way, which leadeth unto life, and few there be that find it" (Matthew 7:13–14). Sadly, in our day there are many who have found it but do not choose it. They know the way is there and where it leads, but they still refuse to commit because it is *so* narrow. Faithful disciples learn the way of Christ is narrow indeed, but never so narrow that He cannot walk it with us. In the end, it is His presence on the covenant path that makes it the only one worth traveling.

My colleague Tyler J. Griffin has pointed out that too

many disciples believe that Christ's infinite Atonement covers everyone else, but not them. Every person must finally say, "*Thou* art the only one who has the power and the love to make *me* clean and whole. In that moment," wrote Brother Griffin, "the infinite Atoner becomes our intimate Savior."[6]

Elder Merrill J. Bateman taught, "The Atonement was not only infinite in its expanse but intimate in the lives of God's children."[7] On another occasion, Elder Bateman said, "For many years I thought of the Savior's experience in the garden and on the cross as places where a large mass of sin was heaped upon Him. Through the words of Alma, Abinadi, Isaiah, and other prophets, however, my view has changed. Instead of an impersonal mass of sin, there was a long line of people, as Jesus felt 'our infirmities' (Hebrews 4:15), '[bore] our griefs, . . . carried our sorrows . . . [and] was bruised for our iniquities' (Isaiah 53:4–5)."[8]

In the Americas, Christ invited the multitudes to come forth "one by one" (3 Nephi 11:15), blessed their children "one by one" (3 Nephi 17:21), and touched and spoke to His disciples "one by one" (3 Nephi 18:36; 28:1). These actions were reminiscent of how He atoned for them—and us—one by one.

Some might ask, "What difference does it make if Christ atoned for us individually or as a group?" For me, it is only in an intimate view of the Atonement that my eternal individuality is validated and preserved. I may only be one of God's numberless children, but I am one. I am a child, not a creation. I am a person, not an object. I am an "I" and not an "it."[9] My immortality and eternal life is God's purpose. He is not using me as a means or stepping-stone to another end. Christ's intimate Atonement is evidence that He has no hidden agenda, no ulterior motive, and no selfish desire to manipulate or use me. It is im-

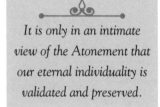

It is only in an intimate view of the Atonement that our eternal individuality is validated and preserved.

possible to love someone deeply without knowing him or her completely. Because the Atonement was intimate, I can trust He loves me wholeheartedly because He knows me so perfectly.

Because of the infinite and eternal sacrifice of the Christ on Calvary, *all* children of God are blessed. Because of the intimate and personal sacrifice of the Christ on Calvary, *each* child of God is blessed. Let us never forget the *us* found in *Jesus*, the *I* found in *Christ*, and the *me* found in *Atonement*.

THE HOLY WEEK
AND THE HOLY CROSS

Our family has always enjoyed Easter. It meant egg coloring, Easter baskets, egg hunts, candy, and sometimes the girls got new dresses. At church, we usually sang "He is Risen!" (*Hymns*, no. 199) and heard wonderful talks and testimonies about the Resurrection of Christ. These are all important traditions and moments of worship. However, it was only when we lived abroad that we realized there were additional aspects of the Easter holiday that could add depth to our celebration and help us better remember the Savior. In Chile, Christians celebrated *la Semana Santa*, or the Holy Week. When my oldest daughter Wendee married an Italian, we admired how seriously he and his family took *Pasqua* or *Settimana Santa* each year. Christians worldwide make efforts to remember the last week of Jesus's life as well as His glorious Resurrection. Our family determined to commemorate in small and simple ways each day of the Holy Week.

On Palm Sunday, we celebrate Jesus's triumphal entry. Scriptures teach us that when the people "heard that Jesus was coming to Jerusalem, [they] took branches of palm trees, and went forth to meet him, and cried, Hosanna: Blessed is the King of Israel" (John 12:12–13). *Hosanna* comes from Hebrew and means "save now" (Bible Dictionary, 661). It was reminiscent of when we shouted for joy before we came to earth because we knew Jesus would be our Savior (see Job 38:7). It was a foreshadowing of what disciples in the Americas would do when Jesus would visit them (see 3 Nephi 4:32) and what we will do when He comes again (see 1 Thessalonians 4:16).

On Cleansing Monday, we remember how Christ sanctified the temple. In Matthew we read, "And Jesus went into the temple of God, and cast out all them that sold and bought in the temple, and overthrew the tables of the moneychangers, and the seats of them that sold doves, and said unto them, It is written, My house shall be called the house of prayer; but ye have made it a den of thieves" (Matthew 21:12–13). Perhaps one of the lessons Jesus was teaching by cleansing the temple was that He has the ability to cleanse us. He can help us rid ourselves of sin and hypocrisy.

On Parable Tuesday, we recall how Jesus taught His disciples: "And the disciples came, and said unto him, Why speakest thou unto them in parables? He answered and said unto them, Because it is given unto you to know the mysteries of the kingdom of heaven, but to them it is not given" (Matthew 13:10–11). Parables are like a picture with hidden objects in it. At first, we see only the obvious picture, but the more we search, the more we find. When Christ taught parables, some people just heard nice stories, but disciples were expected to search harder and find deeper meanings.

Betrayal Wednesday is when we ponder offering and receiving forgiveness. In Luke 22 we read, "Then entered Satan into Judas surnamed Iscariot, being of the number of the twelve. And he went his way, and communed with the chief priests and captains, how he might betray him unto them" (vv. 3–4). Jesus trusted Judas, but Judas betrayed Him. Although Judas's choice led to Christ's arrest, trial, and suffering at the hands of leaders and soldiers, it is not why Jesus suffered. He could have stopped it. He chose to permit it and endure it out of love. He did not do it *because* of Judas, but *for* Judas and all of us. When the soldiers nailed Him to the cross, Jesus said, "Father, forgive them; for they know not what they do" (Luke 23:34). When others hurt us, we can learn to forgive by turning our angry and bitter feelings over to God and trusting Him to deal with the situation.

Last Supper Thursday gives us an opportunity to think about the sacrament and Gethsemane, but it is fascinating to realize that Jesus and His Apostles were actually commemorating the Jewish holiday known as the Passover. It was a time to remember when Egyptian sons ended up dying, but the Israelites' sons were spared because they followed the command to sacrifice a lamb and mark their doorways with the blood. Death passed over their houses (see Exodus 12:23). Did Christ's Apostles yet realize that the event they celebrated foreshadowed what would happen to Jesus in the next few days? Did they understand that God was going to sacrifice His firstborn son Jesus and that through His atoning blood, shed in Gethsemane and on the cross, we can all escape spiritual and physical death?

On Good Friday, we commemorate Christ's Crucifixion. It is difficult at first to understand why we call the day Christ was crucified "good." However, on Good Friday we celebrate everything good and holy that we enjoy or hope to enjoy because of Christ. Most children like to celebrate Christmas more than Easter because they would rather focus on Jesus's birth than His death. Nevertheless, Jesus was born to die. We sing, "For Jesus died on Calvary, That all thru him might ransomed be" (Hymns, no. 177). From the day of His birth, Jesus was preparing to suffer and die on the cross. His death was necessary to bring about the glad tidings of great joy proclaimed at His birth.

On Salvation Saturday, we think of the Savior's visit to the spirit world while His body was in the tomb. In the Doctrine and Covenants, we read the vision of President Joseph F. Smith: "And there were gathered together in one place an innumerable company of the spirits of the just, who had been faithful in the testimony of Jesus while they lived in mortality. . . . I beheld that they were filled with joy and gladness, and were rejoicing together because the day of their deliverance was at hand" (D&C 138:12, 15). In the spirit world, there were also many spirits who had not known of Jesus while they lived on earth. They had not learned the gospel or been baptized. Instead of teaching them directly, Jesus delegated authority and organized the spirits who had already made covenants with Him to visit and prepare the others for baptismal and temple covenants. He called them to be missionaries and carry the light of the gospel to all who were in darkness (see D&C 138:29–30). In this way, Jesus gave everyone who has been or will ever be born the chance to learn faith, repent, accept covenants, and progress.

Finally, on Easter Sunday, we celebrate the Resurrection: "But Mary stood without at the sepulchre weeping. . . . Jesus saith unto her, Woman, why weepest thou? whom seekest thou? She, supposing him to be the gardener, saith unto him, Sir, if thou have borne him hence, tell me where thou hast laid him, and I will take him away. Jesus saith unto her, Mary. She turned herself, and saith unto him, Rabboni; which is to say, Master" (John 20:11, 15–16). Because Jesus came back to life, we will also be resurrected.

My daughter Wendee wrote a wonderful book called *The Holy Week for Latter-day Saint Families*, in which she shared activities families could do to broaden their celebrations of Easter.[1] One suggestion for Good Friday was to make paper plate models of Calvary. Children can cut out a half-circle in the center of their plates and fold the flap to make a hill. Then they can color rocks and grass on the hill. Finally, they can cut out three brown paper crosses to tape on top to remind them of the crosses on which Jesus and the two thieves were crucified.

One mother wrote Wendee a letter and said she did not feel comfortable doing an activity involving the cross. She wrote, "We do not use the cross because it reminds us of Christ's death and we worship a living Christ."

This sister's words echoed the words of President Gordon B. Hinckley, who said something similar when a Protestant minister once interviewed him. The minister asked, "If you do not use the cross, what is the symbol of your religion?" President Hinckley responded, "The lives of our people must become the most meaningful expression of our faith and, in fact, therefore, the symbol of our worship."[2]

It is true that Latter-day Saints do not typically display crosses in homes, chapels, and temples as we strive to make our lives living symbols of our living Lord. However, that does not mean that the cross is not part of our doctrine. We believe that through the "suff'rings sore, endured for us on Calvary, . . . salvation [was] purchased on that tree" (*Hymns*, no. 178). Many Christians downplay the events of Gethsemane when they speak of the Atonement. We must not make the same mistake in reverse by downplaying, over-looking, or devaluing the cross. Latter-day Saint scholars Fiona and Terryl Givens explained further, "In the Garden of Gethsemane, Christ bore the brunt of the Atonement in solitude without [earthly witnesses]. . . . The final manifes-tation of Christ's absolute love, however, had to be a public sacrifice, that the perfect offering might be witnessed, and therefore engulf us and transform us."[3] When writing on the same topic, Latter-day Saint scholar Robert L. Millet reminded, "Scores of passages in the Book of Mormon and modern scripture speak of the vital need for Christ's suffer-ing *and death* . . . on the cruel cross of Calvary—that was an indispensable element of the atoning sacrifice."[4]

More recently, my colleague John Hilton III completed an analysis of the scriptures documenting that the Bible, Book of Mormon, and Doctrine and Covenants each place a stronger emphasis on the Crucifixion than Gethsemane. Across the standard works there are about fifty more scrip-tures that explicitly connect Christ's death on the cross with our salvation than His suffering in Gethsemane (see, for example, 1 Nephi 11:32–33; Mosiah 15:7–9; Alma 21:9; 3 Nephi 27:14; D&C 18:11; 21:9; 35:2; 53:2; 76:41; 138:35). Similarly, Brother Hilton examined what Church leaders have taught about Gethsemane and the Crucifixion in the *Journal of Discourses* and general conference. He found that Church leaders have mentioned Christ's Crucifixion much more frequently than they have Gethsemane and in recent years have often mentioned Christ's Crucifixion in connection with Gethsemane.[5]

Latter-day Saints understand it is not a competition between the two sites. We know that both were vital parts of the Atonement and deserve our honor, respect, and reverence. Elder Tad R. Callister defined the Atonement as "a series of divine events that commenced in the Garden of Gethsemane, continued on the cross, and culminated with the Savior's Resurrection from the tomb."[6] President Russell M. Nelson taught, "In the Garden of Gethsemane, our Savior took upon Himself *every* pain, *every* sin, and *all* of the anguish and suffering *ever* experienced by you and me and by everyone who has ever lived or will ever live. . . . All of this suffering was intensified as He was cruelly crucified on Calvary's cross. Through these excruciating experiences and His subsequent Resurrection—His infinite Atonement—He granted immortality to all and ransomed each one of us."[7]

Because of the Christ on Calvary, we honor the cross. However, we also honor Gethsemane and the empty tomb. We celebrate the Resurrection of the Lord on Easter Sunday, but as we also ponder all that happened during the final week of Christ's mortal life, we more fully keep our promise to "always remember him" (Moroni 4:3).

FIVE SCRIPTURES
I USED TO DISLIKE,
BUT NOW I LOVE

People sometimes list foods or activities they once disliked but now they love: tomatoes, spinach, gardening, or doing family history. One item on my list is what we used to call typing. When I was younger, I struggled to do it well. My children tease me because they found out my lowest grade at Brigham Young University was in Beginning Typewriting. They do not know what is funnier, that there was a university-level class in typewriting or that their dad did so poorly in it. Of course, now I use the keyboard all the time and am quite proficient at it.

I went through a similar shift with some scriptures. I was never a fan of Isaiah until much later in my life. I did not like Zenos's allegory in Jacob 5, but now I love it. I used to call Acts through Revelation the sealed portion of the New Testament, but now I love it. Most of the Old Testament was in the dislike column, but more and more parts are finding their way to the love column. With those confessions out of the way, let me share five specific verses I disliked when I was younger but now I love. Coming to understand each one better has helped me appreciate the depth and breadth of Christ's Atonement.

First, in Isaiah 53:10–11 (see also Mosiah 14:10–11) we read, "Yet it pleased the Lord to bruise him. . . . He shall see of the travail of his soul, and shall be satisfied." To me those words made Heavenly Father sound mean. What kind of Father is "pleased" because of His Son's suffering and "satisfied" because of His Son's anguish? Later, I read the same verses in the New Revised Standard Version of the Bible. This translation, published in 1989, relies heavily upon the King James Version but also uses the Dead Sea Scrolls and other records that were not available when the King James Version was completed. The NRSV's more literal translation of Isaiah 53:10–11 reads, "Yet it was the will of the Lord to crush him. . . . Out of his anguish he shall see light; . . . he shall find satisfaction through his knowledge." The new rendering helped me see that Christ's suffering did not make God happy, but it was still His will, because through Christ's anguish we could all receive light. This knowledge brought God great satisfaction. Similarly, we read that Jesus is our "advocate with the Father" (1 John 2:1; D&C 29:5; 32:3), and the phrase conjures up images of a kind and loving Jesus pleading in our behalf before an angry and condemning Father in Heaven, as if Christ is "our shield and defender

31

against the wrath and vengeance of a sovereign God."[1] This view is not a fair representation of our Father. Perhaps we should think of the words "with the Father" as meaning *along with* the Father rather than *before* the Father. Such an interpretation makes more sense to me, since Jesus, not the Father, will be our ultimate judge (see Romans 14:10; Moroni 8:21; D&C 135:5). Fiona and Terryl Givens wrote, "Christ is not protecting us from divine anger or judgment. On the contrary, Christ is collaborating with our Heavenly Parents for our homecoming."[2] Had God the Father been able to die for us, He would have. But He already had an immortal body and could not die. It had to be Jesus. How pleased God must have been that Christ was willing to do for us what He could not. How satisfied Heavenly Father and Mother must have felt that Jesus was willing to save us.

Second, Alma 42:13 states, "The work of justice could not be destroyed; if so, God would cease to be God." I never liked this verse when I was younger because it seemed like God was not in charge. I figured that if God had to yield to the law of justice then He must be a weakling. Shouldn't God be able to change the law, stand up to it, or at least grant a few executive pardons? Greater perspective came as I learned that God is God not only because He gives the law (see D&C 88:42) but also because He obeys it. If He removed the law, He would destroy the moral order of the universe and invite chaos. Conforming to the law is how God preserves our freedom. The Book of Mormon clarifies that justice is not an inflexible principle that exists independent of God. Rather, it is one of His attributes, just like mercy. If either attribute could override the other, it would limit freedom (see 2 Nephi 2; Alma 41–42).[3] The law of jus-

tice demands our immediate perfection or a consequence. Because Jesus took that consequence, the disrupted scales were balanced and order was restored. He and God could mercifully ask for our even-

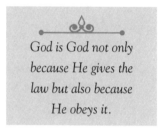

God is God not only because He gives the law but also because He obeys it.

tual perfection and offer Their divine assistance. I love this verse now because I realize that during the Atonement, Jesus conformed to God's will and God conformed to the law to safeguard our freedom.

Third, in Matthew 26:39 we read Christ's plea in Gethsemane: "And he went a little further, and fell on his face, and prayed, saying, O my Father, if it be possible, let this cup pass from me." This phrase saddened me when I was younger because it sounded like Christ was backing down. I reasoned that if Jesus had always been about His "Father's business" (Luke 2:49) and even testified to Pilate, "To this end was I born, and for this cause came I into the world" (John 18:37), then why was He now unwilling to proceed? Did He not love us? It was Elder Neal A. Maxwell's words that helped me understand: "In Gethsemane the suffering

Jesus began to be 'sore amazed' (Mark 14:33), or, in the Greek, 'awestruck' and 'astonished.' Imagine, Jehovah, the Creator of this and other worlds, 'astonished'! Jesus knew cognitively what He must do, but not experientially. He had never personally known the exquisite and exacting process of such an atonement before. Thus, when the agony came in its fullness, it was so much, much worse than even He with His unique intellect had ever imagined!"[4] Now, I love this scripture because it makes me feel "awestruck" and "astonished" that Christ did not quit. It is because He loved us that He proceeded even though it was difficult. I feel similar to President Gordon B. Hinckley when he said, "Through giving His life in pain and unspeakable suffering, He has reached down to lift me. . . . My gratitude knows no bounds. My thanks to my Lord has no conclusion."[5]

Fourth, when Jesus entered Gethsemane, He invited Peter, James, and John to "tarry" and "watch with [Him]" (Matthew 26:38), but they fell asleep. Christ asked, "Could ye not watch with me one hour?" (v. 40). These scriptures made me feel disappointed in the Apostles for not supporting Christ. In my youth, it was easy to judge and condemn these Apostles. However, the older I grew, the more I related to the Apostles. How many small and simple things has Christ asked of me? How many times have I let Him down? Now I love the scripture because it highlights the human condition for which Christ atoned for us in the first place. The fact that Peter, James, and John fell short—multiple times—demonstrates how desperately we all needed Christ to do for us what we could not do for ourselves. Sister Chieko Okazaki, former Counselor in the Relief Society General Presidency, said, "[Christ is] not waiting for us to be perfect. Perfect people don't need a Savior. He came to save us in our imperfections. He is the Lord of the living, and the living make mistakes. He's not embarrassed by us, angry at us, or shocked. He wants us in our brokenness, in our unhappiness, in our guilt and our grief."[6]

Fifth, Matthew 27:46 tells us that when Christ was on the cross, He "cried with a loud voice, saying, . . . My God, my God, why hast thou forsaken me?" When I was younger, I disliked this scripture for two reasons: 1) I could not understand why God would leave Jesus alone in the moment He needed Him the most, and 2) The forlorn words seemed like an admission of defeat before the Jews. The Jews wanted a Messiah to save them from Rome and surely saw Christ's death as evidence that He failed. Why, I wondered, would Christ not set them straight and declare to them that His death was a victory?

It helped me to learn that in order to descend below all things (see D&C 88:6; Ephesians 4:9–10) and tread "the wine-press alone" (D&C 76:107), the Savior had to be "left alone by His Father" and complete the Atonement "of His own free will and choice."[7] "He had to feel what it was like to die not only physically but spiritually."[8] That perspective let me see God's withdrawal as necessary. I love how completely God trusted Jesus. He knew that even without His presence or the help of the Spirit or angels or anyone, Christ would endure and prevail.

However, I truly came to love this scripture when I learned the Jews would not have heard Christ's words as an admission of defeat, but as a proclamation of victory. Christ was quoting scripture.[9] The first line of Psalm 22 is "My God, my God, why hast thou forsaken me?" My colleague Shon Hopkin wrote, "Christ was not simply fulfilling prophecy and expressing his feelings of loss while hanging on the cross but, in addition, was still lovingly teaching his people by communicating to them the many concepts contained in Psalm 22—including his final victory over suffering—while uttering only one short phrase."[10] By quoting this phrase, Christ reminded listeners that His suffering and death were foreknown and that everything was unfolding exactly as it should. All those familiar with Psalm 22 would have instantly recognized what Christ was saying because the opening line "would have connected the statement with the entire psalm, much as Latter-day Saints who hear the phrase 'Come, come, ye Saints' will immediately recall the tune and the following line[s]."[11]

Despite the intense suffering Christ was enduring on the cross, He was teaching of His divine Sonship (see Psalm

22:9–10). Soldiers had pierced His hands and feet (v. 16) and cast lots for His garment (v. 18), but He would soon begin the work in the "great congregation" of the spirit world (v. 25). Then He would be resurrected, and "all the ends of the world shall remember and turn unto the Lord: and all the kindreds of the nations shall worship" (v. 27). Although Jesus hung dying before them now, He was reminding them that He would ultimately stand victoriously at the head of His kingdom and as the Governor of all nations forever (see v. 28).

Because of the Christ on Calvary, God was pleased and satisfied in the knowledge that His children could be saved. Christ conformed to God's will as God conformed to the law to preserve freedom that is essential for our happiness and progress. Even though Christ's suffering was worse than He had previously understood, He still endured it because of His perfect love for us. We regularly fail to wait one hour with Him, but His "grace is sufficient . . . [and His] strength is made perfect in weakness" (2 Corinthians 12:9). Because the Christ on Calvary suffered alone, we will never have to. His death was not the end, but the beginning. His Resurrection was a victory. Because of the Christ on Calvary, His—and our—ultimate triumph is secure. With the prophet Jacob I ask, "Why not speak of the atonement of Christ"? (Jacob 4:12).

EASTER'S PRIVILEGES

The Miracles of Christ's Atonement

Surprisingly, Romans 5:11 is the only verse in the entire New Testament in which we read the word *Atonement*: "We . . . joy in God through our Lord Jesus Christ, by whom we have now received the atonement." All Christians agree Christ has given us a great gift, but some may not fully understand the extent of the gift. Let us reflect on sacred privileges and blessings that are ours because of the Atonement of Jesus Christ: resurrection, repentance, consolation and healing, and transformation.

Although I present these privileges separately, they are not isolated and distinct from one another. They actually combine and interact on multiple levels. It can be difficult to see where one ends and the others begin. Nevertheless, looking at each individually can allow us to reflect on the miracles of Christ's Atonement.

A TALE OF TWO TOMBS

In 1917, British archeologist and Egyptologist Howard Carter was hired to supervise excavations in Egypt. By 1922, his employer was discouraged with the lack of results and gave Howard only one more year to make a significant discovery or he would find himself without funding. Howard considered digging in new locations, but instead returned to a site he had abandoned several years earlier. This time he dug deeper. It was then that his team unearthed a staircase leading to a sealed door. On November 26, 1922, Howard chiseled away a corner of the door and, by candlelight, peered into a tomb filled with gold and ebony.

"Can you see anything?" someone asked.

Howard replied, "Yes, wonderful things!" He had discovered the tomb of Tutankhamun, commonly known as King Tut.

Contrast Howard's experience with that of two Apostles, John and Peter, who "ran both together" (John

20:4) to the tomb of Jesus on the first Easter morning. John, who reached the tomb before Peter, stooped down and looked inside. Can you imagine their conversation when Peter arrived, before they entered? (see vv. 5–6). Peter may have asked, "Can you see anything?" Then, unlike Howard Carter, John may have responded, "No, nothing except the linen in which the Lord's body was wrapped." King Tut's tomb was full of "wonderful things." Jesus's tomb was empty—the most wonderful thing of all.

Elder D. Todd Christofferson testified, "The Resurrection confirms the divinity of Jesus Christ and the reality of God the Father."[1] Because Jesus rose from the dead, we will all live after we die.

Although many Christians believe in a type of resurrection, not all believe that our spirits will actually reunite with our bodies for eternity as Latter-day Saints do (see 2 Nephi 9:12; Alma 11:42).[2] Many believe God is a spirit, so such a reunion seems unnecessary and undesirable to them. We might ask, as did Latter-day Saint scholar Truman G. Madsen, "Why would an unembodied God create an embodied man to achieve a disembodied immortality?" With Brother Madsen, we testify God did not: "The body is the crowning stage of progressive unfoldment toward celestial [glory]."[3] It is only when our spirits are connected eternally with our resurrected bodies that we will "receive a fulness of joy" (D&C 93:33).

Paul testified that he saw the resurrected Christ (see 1 Corinthians 15:4–8). Additionally, he taught that our resurrections will take place at different times and be to different degrees of glory: "There are also celestial bodies, and bodies terrestrial: but the glory of the celestial is one, and the glory of the terrestrial is another. There is one glory of the sun, and another glory of the moon, and another glory of the stars: for one star differeth from another star in glory. So also is the resurrection of the dead" (1 Corinthians 15:40–42).

In Doctrine and Covenants 76, we read that those who receive both a testimony of Christ and—as demonstrated by making and keeping covenants—the gospel of Christ (see vv. 50, 69) shall be resurrected with celestial glory (see v. 50). Next will be those who receive a testimony of Jesus but reject the gospel and its covenants even after they are offered (see v. 73). They will be resurrected with terrestrial glory (see v. 78). Following will be those who, despite having had every opportunity, do not accept "the gospel of Christ, neither the testimony of Jesus" (v. 82). They will be telestial. Finally, the sons and daughters of perdition will come forth—those who not only reject Christ and His gospel but also choose to rebel against them (see v. 35).[4]

One young Latter-day Saint man asked me, "If the Resurrection is real, why did they find the bodies of King Tut and all those other pharaohs when they discovered their

43

tombs? They lived before Jesus, so wouldn't they have been resurrected when He was?"

I explained that they would have been if they had been ready for a celestial resurrection, but Jesus did not open the way for the gospel to be taught in the spirit world until after His Crucifixion, while His body was in the tomb (see D&C 138). King Tut and his friends still had much to learn. There were others who were prepared for celestial glory and came forth soon after Jesus: "Father Adam . . . and our glorious Mother Eve, with many of her faithful daughters who had lived through the ages and worshiped the true and living God" (D&C 138:38–39). The list included Abel, Seth, Noah, Shem, Abraham, Isaac, Jacob, Moses, and more (see vv. 40–41). In the Americas, additional Saints came forth and appeared and ministered to many (see 3 Nephi 23:9–10). Still others have been resurrected since that time. Moroni, for example, died about four hundred years after Christ (see Mormon 8:24; Moroni 10:2), but came to Joseph Smith in 1823 as a resurrected being (see the introduction to the Book of Mormon).

The vast majority of God's children are still spirits in the spirit world getting ready—and helping others get ready—to "abide a celestial glory" (D&C 88:22). Those who reach that point by the Second Coming will be resurrected then. Others will come forth throughout the Millennium as their temple work is completed. Those who have every opportunity to learn the fullness of the gospel but refuse vicarious ordinances will come forth at the end of the Millennium (terrestrial) or after the Millennium (telestial and sons and daughters of perdition). Each spirit will receive a body to match the faith that has been developed by his or her spirit throughout premortal, mortal, and postmortal experiences.

When the doctrine of various kingdoms of glory was first revealed to Joseph Smith and Sidney Rigdon (see D&C 76), it caused quite a stir among the Saints. Some were thrilled to learn the full truth, as the traditional Christian idea of meeting God the moment we die and being immediately assigned to heaven or hell had seemed too simplistic to them. Others angrily apostatized because they felt like the doctrine made heaven too easy for people to attain and God too merciful.[5]

More revelations followed explaining that essential ordinances could be performed for those who had passed away. Once again, the doctrine was divisive. Some Saints rushed to the Mississippi River and began baptizing each other for deceased loved ones immediately.[6] They were overjoyed to realize that Jesus's grace could extend to countless people on the other side of the veil who had died without a covenant relationship with Him. Other people were upset. They believed that "this life is the time for men to prepare to meet God" (Alma 34:32) and refused to accept that the spirit world, which is on this same earth, could be seen as an extension of "this life."[7]

Regardless of the different responses, Joseph continued to teach the Saints about the afterlife and resurrection because he knew these understandings were essential in helping them understand God's true character and grasp their eternal potential. He explained, "Our heavenly Father is more liberal in His views, and boundless in His mercies and blessings, than we are ready to believe or receive."[8] On another occasion, the Prophet taught, "Although the earthly tabernacle shall be dissolved, they shall rise in immortal glory . . . [and] shall be heirs of God and joint-heirs with Jesus Christ."[9] In Doctrine and Covenants 132 we read, "Ye shall come forth in the first [celestial] resurrection; . . . and shall inherit thrones, kingdoms, principalities, and powers, dominions, all heights and depths. . . . Then shall [ye] be gods" (vv. 19–20). Joseph never suggested this journey would be quick or easy. On the contrary, he made it clear that "the process would take time, requiring much patience, faith, and learning." He said, "It is not all to be comprehended in this world. It will take a long time after the grave to understand the whole."[10] Nevertheless, he assured the Saints that celestial glory awaits all those who enter a covenant relationship with Christ in mortality or in the spirit world as they accept proxy ordinances done in their behalf. "It is no more incredible," the Prophet said, "that God should *save* the dead, than that he should *raise* the dead."[11] When Joseph taught this doctrine, it was received the same way previous revelations had been. Some rejoiced, while others claimed he was a fallen prophet and plotted his death.[12]

Today, many people still reject Joseph's revelations, but I am thankful to belong to a church with a heaven that is larger than its hell. I am happy to worship a successful Savior who will take us as far as we are willing to go.

No one chooses a glory on a whim or in a moment. This decision will be made much like our initial choice to follow Christ in the premortal existence. Latter-day Saint scholar Robert J. Matthews taught, "The grand council in heaven was probably a series of meetings that could have lasted thousands of years. The idea that we were spirits roaming around who then held one meet-

I am thankful to belong to a church with a heaven that is larger than its hell. I am happy to worship a successful Savior who will take us as far as we are willing to go.

ing and had one vote is too simplified. We were taught for centuries. Those who became the devil and his angels did not become that way through a vote, but a life-style. You don't become 'perdition' through one bad vote."[13] In the same way, you do not become celestial through one good vote. We will choose the glory of our resurrected bodies and thus our kingdoms of glory by our lifestyles.

Resurrection is not *the* final judgment (or we could say *placement* in our eternal kingdoms[14]). Christ and His Apostles will one day judge us much like members of bishoprics and stake presidencies interview us and sign our temple recommends now (see 1 Nephi 12:9; 2 Timothy 4:1). However, we also act as our "own judges" (Alma 41:7) as we sign our own recommends. When we chose to come to earth to obtain a body in the first place, we acted as our own judges. As we choose to make and keep covenants, we act as our own judges. When we choose the glory of our resurrected bodies and eternal kingdoms, we act as our own judges. Alma taught, "The one raised to happiness according to his desires of happiness, or good according to his desires of good; and the other to evil according to his desires of evil" (Alma 41:5).

> As we choose to make and keep covenants, we act as our own judges.

Thankfully, no final judgments or placements will happen until after we all have time to prepare and educate our desires. In the spirit world, "worthy and qualified messengers" teach others and help them prepare to make and keep covenants just as "worthy and qualified messengers" do in mortality.[15] Paul wrote, "God . . . will have all men to be saved, and to come unto the knowledge of the truth" (1 Timothy 2:3–4). President Joseph F. Smith wrote, "Jesus had not finished his work when his body was slain, neither did he finish it after his resurrection from the dead, although he had accomplished the purpose for which he then came to the earth, he had not fulfilled all his work. And when will he? Not until he has redeemed and saved every son and daughter of our father."[16] In this life and the spirit world, the Lord works "with his power . . . among the children of men, extending the arm of mercy towards them that put their trust in him" (Mosiah 29:20). Heavenly Father and Jesus will not rest until everyone has had every possible opportunity. They are not waiting for us to fail, but giving us every chance to succeed.

That said, the fact that many opportunities are given doesn't justify our procrastination. We cannot "confuse an open door with automatic admission."[17] One struggling returned missionary said, "If it turns out there really is a God and a plan of salvation, I'll just repent in the spirit world."

I responded, "Great idea, except for one thing. If the knowledge you have now does not give you the desire to change and draw closer to God, what makes you think the knowledge you have then will?"

He said, "It's just too hard now. It will be easier then."

I asked, "Was middle school

> *Heavenly Father and Jesus will not rest until everyone has had every possible opportunity. They are not waiting for us to fail, but giving us every chance to succeed.*

easier than elementary school? Was high school easier than middle school?"

"No," he responded.

"Then what makes you think the next phase of our preparation will be easier than the previous one?" Elder James E. Talmage wrote, "As the time of repentance is procrastinated, the ability to repent grows weaker; neglect of opportunity in holy things develops inability."[18] This is not because God limits us but because we limit ourselves. A habit of apathy and procrastination can easily become part of our character.

So what hope is there? The answer is the enduring love of family and the irresistible grace of Christ. President Thomas S. Monson reminded us that during Christ's mortal ministry, His "forgiveness was unbounded, his patience inexhaustible, his courage without limit. Jesus changed men. He changed their habits, their opinions, their ambitions. He changed their tempers, their dispositions, their natures. He changed men's hearts."[19] If He did it for them, He can do it for us, as we are willing.

Paul taught, "Be not weary in well doing" (2 Thessalonians 3:13). When we finally come forth with celestial bodies, it will be worth it. We will pass through the veil and God will, as President Brigham Young taught, "embrace [us] and say, 'My son, my daughter, I have you again;' and [we will] say, 'O my Father, my Father, I am here again.'"[20] This reunion will be joyous not just because we will have come home, but because we will have become enough like Him to feel at home.

Because Jesus loosed the bands of death (see Alma 11:42) and was the first to be resurrected (see 1 Corinthians 15:23), we will all be resurrected. "Our flesh must waste away and die; nevertheless, in our bodies we shall see God" (2 Nephi 9:4). Because of the Christ on Calvary, we will all survive mortality. Because of the Christ on Calvary, we are free to do with our immortality as much as we desire.

When Howard Carter chiseled away the entrance to King Tut's tomb, he saw "wonderful things." Apostles found Jesus's tomb empty, but "Eye hath not seen, nor ear heard, neither have entered into the heart of man, the things which God hath prepared for them that love him" (1 Corinthians 2:9). Because of the Christ on Calvary, "the end" can be replaced with "and they lived happily ever after."

REPENTANCE: CLEAR AS CRYSTAL

Crystal grew up just outside of St. Louis, Missouri. Her parents both worked to make ends meet, and her siblings fought a lot, so she did not really enjoy being at home. She struggled to make friends at church, so she always felt like an outcast there. It wasn't long before she started seeking belonging in all the wrong places. Her freshman year she started smoking, drinking, and partying. Looking back, she told me, "I never was too comfortable in that crowd either. I was too good for the world and too bad for the Church. I just didn't seem to fit anywhere."

At age seventeen, Crystal moved out, was arrested for shoplifting, and got suspended from school for a time. She got a job at a fast-food restaurant and was surprised one day when two elders showed up. She did not know if they were there to eat or if her mom had sent them to save her. Either way, they offered to meet with her and teach her the lessons. It was a turning point.

Crystal graduated from high school and joined the navy. Friends and family threw a farewell party for her before she went to boot camp. The next day, she arrived at the deployment station ready to leave and was told she had not reached her target weight and would have to lose six more pounds and come back in two months. Crystal was embarrassed. How could she face her friends and family when she felt like she had failed—again? She was angry with the people at the deployment station, angry with herself, and angry with God.

Not wanting to go home, she went on a long walk. "Okay, God," she prayed. "Let's have this out! What am I supposed to do now? I've been trying to improve and this is what I get? This is my blessing? I've been killing myself to lose weight and you couldn't help me lose six more pounds?"

I interrupt this regularly scheduled story to bring you a lesson: It is easy to see what Crystal did wrong, but let us focus on what she did right. Crystal turned to God and was honest with Him. At a moment when many people would have run away from God, Crystal ran to Him. She poured her heart out about her disappointment, but she also prayed to Him about what the missionaries had been teaching her. She prayed about Joseph Smith ("Was he a liar?") and the Book of Mormon ("Could a young man fabricate such a story?"). She prayed about whether or not the Church is true and what that meant for her ("If those early Saints were doing what's right and still faced hardships, then what am I supposed to learn from this?").

At the end of that long walk and long prayer, Crystal realized she had the beginnings of her testimony. The next two months turned out to be a blessing rather than a curse. Crystal started reading the Book of Mormon regularly. She went back to church. Crystal still had her struggles, but she chose to deal with them in the Church rather than out of it. Repentance is not about getting our acts together so we can go to church. We go to church to help us get our acts together. God "cannot look upon sin with the least degree of allowance" (Alma 45:16), but He can look upon sinners who are trying to improve with a lot of patience.[1] Crystal began the process of quitting her bad habits and losing more weight. She started listening to talks by Church speakers. Her mom had bought the recordings to try to motivate Crystal when she was younger. Now she finally wanted to listen. "It sounds weird," she told me, "but it was like I developed friendships with the speakers. I knew their voices and almost memorized their talks. The messages seemed like they were just for me."

Looking back, Crystal is grateful that she was not allowed to leave when she wanted. She explained, "If I had entered the navy without that additional spiritual strength, I wonder if I would have been able to resist the temptations I faced—especially considering my past. Those two months were pivotal in my life, like an MTC that prepared me for the future. I realized I did not have to feel like a second-class citizen in the Church because of my past. I had a lot to learn, but that did not keep me from having a testimony, praying, and participating."

Two months and six pounds later, Crystal was off to boot camp. No friends, church, or recorded talks allowed there. Crystal said, "I would have been lonely, but I was too tired. When I felt like giving up, I prayed for strength. In my mind, I would replay the Church talks. Those speakers had no idea they were helping me do pushups and run obstacle courses, but there they were in my mind, cheering me on. When the Recruit Division Commanders were yelling in my face, I would remind myself that I am a beloved child of God and His opinion is the only one that matters."

What did Crystal do right? She realized that repentance is not just about stopping bad things, but starting good things. It is not just about asking God for His forgiveness, but also for His help.

Crystal's first duty station was Pearl Harbor, Hawaii. She was on sea duty and would deploy for months at a time. The sailors were crude. When they found out

> *Repentance is not just about stopping bad things, but starting good things.*

she was a member of the Church they figured that meant she was a virgin and teased her mercilessly. "That was a bad day," Crystal recalled. "There are not a lot of places to hide on a ship." She had her circle of friends, but got tired of seeing them turn into completely different people at each port of call when they would go to bars and get drunk. "I would retreat to my bunk and pull out the recordings my mother had sent, and my Church speakers would tell me it is okay to be different and I'm never alone."

"Looking back," Crystal recounted, "the navy wasn't all bad. I traveled the world. Wherever we were in port, I looked up the Church and met the nicest people who went out of their way to take me to meetings or make sure I got the sacrament."

Late one night, Crystal was alone on the deck in the middle of the ocean looking up at millions of stars. She marveled at the immensity of the universe. The Spirit whispered, "God did all of this for you." Right then she felt as if she were the only one on earth and Heavenly Father had nothing better to do right then than be near her. She thought of Christ's Atonement, and the Spirit whispered, "Christ did it all for you." Crystal said, "These were epiphanies that were huge game-changers for me." That night she knew the love of God and the Savior were as vast as the universe above her and as deep as the ocean beneath her. She finally found where she belonged.

Lesson break: God did not love Crystal because she was good, but because He is good. Christ did not love her because she deserved or earned it, but because she is His. Her repentance was not motivated by guilt, rewards, or duty, but out of love. In Alma 37:9 we read a definition of repentance that is often overlooked: Repentance is being brought "to the knowledge of the Lord [our] God, and to rejoice in Jesus Christ [our] Redeemer."[2] This is what Crystal experienced.

Back at Pearl Harbor, she attended her ward and prepared to enter the temple. She spoke with her bishop and soon received her endowment and became a temple worker.

What did Crystal do right? She turned to her bishop. Bishops have the keys to help us. They can validate our progress and encourage us to keep moving toward positive goals. It is no surprise that Crystal's changes sparked a strong desire to go to the temple. After the people in the Americas heard Christ's voice in the darkness (see 3 Nephi 9:13), they gathered at the temple. They spoke of the "great and marvelous change which had taken place" (3 Nephi 11:1). It was probably not just the dramatic change in the landscape, but also the change Christ had caused within them.[3] Crystal also had experienced that great and marvelous change.

Crystal served for seven years in the navy. Four years later, she met and married Marc. "I waited a long time for marriage," Crystal said, "but Marc was definitely worth the wait!" They were married in the Draper Utah Temple and now have two beautiful girls. Happy ending? Crystal says,

"Absolutely! However, trials and temptations continue. Life is full of ups and downs. We never run out of things to pray about. This is mortality, after all. I still do dumb things, but I keep trying. My past does not condemn my future. I just keep clinging to my family and the Savior and staying on the covenant path."

One last lesson: Repentance is never over. Like washing your hands, it has to happen constantly.[4] However, repentance is about more than cleanliness. Elder Bruce C. Hafen and Marie K. Hafen wrote, "The Atonement is fundamentally a doctrine of human development, not a doctrine that simply erases black marks."[5] Development is not a quick process. Christ Himself never claimed to be perfect until He was resurrected (see 3 Nephi 12:48), so we have a long way to go. The Greek word for perfect, finished, or complete is *teleios*,[6] similar to *telephone*, *television*, and *telescope*—communication and vision at a distance. Perfection is a distant goal. Repentance is not getting back to perfect, since none of us started there. Repentance is growing toward perfection. It is not a punishment for slipping from perfection, but progress in that direction.

> *Repentance is not getting back to perfect, since none of us started there. Repentance is growing toward perfection.*

Crystal told me, "I feel that enough time has passed that the mistakes of my youth are just that.

I was the daughter who sent my parents to bed crying. Now my parents and I are best friends." Repentance is one of the greatest gifts we have been given. Elder Dieter F. Uchtdorf taught, "True repentance is not about shame. It is about becoming. . . . One of the great reasons why we wanted so desperately to come to this earth [was] to learn the lessons of failing and of feeling the blessings, peace, and refining influence of repentance and the miracle of forgiveness."[7]

Because of the Christ on Calvary, we can accept God's invitation to help us grow. Because of the Christ on Calvary, self-hatred can become self-improvement. Guilt can become peace. Regret can become learning. Because of the Christ on Calvary, we can find where we belong, and that is as clear as Crystal!

TO RUN TO OUR AID

My friend Jennifer Reeder has spoken at Time Out for Women events where I have also presented. Her books, *The Witness of Women*,[1] which relates firsthand experiences from the Restoration, and *At the Pulpit*,[2] which reviews 185 years of discourses by our sisters, have highlighted the lives and testimonies of Latter-day Saint women throughout history. Now I want to highlight Jenny.

Jenny was diagnosed with leukemia in 2010 and spent the next two years going through intense chemo treatments. Finally, she was told she was in remission. In 2013, she graduated with her PhD from George Mason University in Virginia and landed her dream job at the Church History Department in Salt Lake City. She bought a home in Utah and was excited to start a new chapter in her life. The only problem was that the earlier chapter was not yet over. Her doctor in Salt Lake did a bone marrow biopsy and found the leukemia was back; her blood was 96 percent leukemic.

She needed a bone marrow transplant. Her siblings wanted to help, but only two were matches—her brothers. Doctors chose Ben, the older of the two, as the best match, and he dropped everything and ran to his sister's aid. He came to Salt Lake from California and prepared for the stem cell transplant.

For two four-hour sessions over two days, Ben had to lie in a bed with his arms extended. Doctors took blood from one arm and then returned it to the other minus the stem cells they needed for Jenny. Ben had to keep his arms completely still, and the process gave him miserable, flu-like symptoms.

Before Jenny could receive the transfusion, she had to go through another round of chemo and total body radiation (with extra to the brain), which left her with a compromised immune system. On November 10, 2013, Jenny had the transplant. She was weak and her esophagus became so inflamed that she could not swallow. Nutrition and liquids came through IVs. For eight weeks she was in the hospital, and for the next three months she could not be more than thirty miles away from it. Her sister cared for her.

Jenny's recovery was slow, and she was off work for a year. Just as she was starting to feel normal again, doctors found more signs of leukemia in her blood. Ben provided another boost of his stem cells, and all was well for a while. Then the leukemia went to her next blood barrier: the bone. Jenny ended up with leukemia lesions on her spine, sternum, and ribs. She was able to fight the cancer off with immunosuppressant treatments for several months, but it kept coming back. Jenny was discouraged and frightened.

Doctors said she needed another transfusion, but they were pessimistic. They told Jenny there was only a four percent chance that it would work. To make matters worse, before they could begin the second transplant, they found that—thanks to having such low immunity—Jenny had contracted pneumonia. Doctors spent three months trying to figure out proper treatment. Jenny was on oxygen with a horrible cough and was in and out of the hospital, including the ICU, before they found the right medicine. During this time, Jenny worried about what was happening with her leukemia. Was it taking over while everyone focused on her pneumonia? She asked her family, friends, and ward to fast and pray for her yet again. Finally, her lungs were clear enough to receive more stem cells, and this time her other brother, Josh, came running to her aid. On April 14, 2017, which happened to be Good Friday, Jenny received her second transplant. Despite the odds, this one was successful. "It was a blessing and a miracle," Jenny told me.

Jenny now has been in remission for over three years. She is grateful for the help she received from her sisters and friends, but she feels especially grateful for her brothers. She said, "Some brothers say they would do anything for you, but my brothers proved it. They gave me my life. No one forced or pressured them. They did it out of love. Their sacrifices for me have created a strong bond between us."

As I heard Jenny's words, I thought of the bond we all have with our Brother Jesus Christ. He promised to do anything for us and proved it. He came running to our aid and gave us our lives. He did not do it because He had to or should. He did it out of love. Jenny's brothers stretched out their arms and gave her their blood. When Christ hung on the cross, He stretched out His arms and gave us His blood. It was a perfect match.

We typically define the Atonement as Christ's suffering in Gethsemane and on the cross and His victory over death. However, taking a broad view, His atoning mission also included His unique birth, sinless life, mortal experiences, and the mocking and pain inflicted upon Him by the Sanhedrin and Romans. Robert L. Millet wrote, "There is a very real sense . . . in which *the Savior's entire life* was a part of His atoning labor."[3]

> *Christ promised to do anything for us and proved it. He came running to our aid and gave us our lives. He did not do it because He had to or should. He did it out of love.*

All of this gave Christ an understanding that goes far beyond empathy alone. Elder David A. Bednar taught, "There is no physical pain, no spiritual wound, no anguish of soul or heartache, no infirmity or weakness you or I ever confront in mortality that the Savior did not experience first."[4]

Our Brother's sacrifice granted us a new life: life after death and the chance to repent and be forgiven of our sins. In addition, the Atonement, completed in the past, opened a door through which Christ can help and heal us in the present. Nephi foresaw Christ's day and wrote, "Behold, they will crucify him; and after he is laid in a sepulchre for the space of three days he shall rise from the dead, with healing in his wings" (2 Nephi 25:13). The German word for Savior is *Heiland.* It is a derivative of the German word *heilen,* which means to heal as well as to save. Terryl and Fiona Givens have assured us that the same connection exists in other languages as well.[5]

I love in 3 Nephi when the Savior said, "Return unto me, . . . that I may heal you" (3 Nephi 9:13). Later, He stated, "Have ye any that are sick among you? Bring them hither" (3 Nephi 17:7). He listed the lame, blind, halt, maimed, leprous, withered, and deaf. Then He extended His invitation to any who were "afflicted in any manner. Bring them [all] hither and I will heal them" (v. 7).

Jenny needed physical healing. Others suffer mentally and emotionally. In our world of pressures and problems, resilience can quickly give way to anxiety, and hope can surrender to despair and depression. No matter the source of our struggles, we plead, "Where can I turn for peace? Where is my solace when other sources cease to make me whole?" (*Hymns*, no. 129). The answer is always the Savior.

Daniel K. Judd, dean of religious education at Brigham Young University, led a research team that studied the mental health of 635 Latter-day Saint university students. Results, published by the American Psychological Association, showed that those who reported understanding and experiencing grace had lower levels of depression, anxiety, perfectionism, and shame.[6]

Alma taught, "And [Christ] will take upon him [our] infirmities, that his bowels may be filled with mercy, according to the flesh, that he may know according to the flesh how to succor his people according to their infirmities" (Alma 7:12). We typically think of the word *succor* as meaning to support and assist. However, the word comes from the Latin *succurrere*, which means to run to our aid.[7] Just as Jenny's brothers ran to her aid, Christ will run to ours. Because of the Christ on Calvary, we can find perfect understanding, inexhaustible grace, and ultimately complete healing.

OUR GOD
WITH US JOINING

Before Easter each spring, many children in the United States celebrate Saint Patrick's Day. They display shamrocks, wear green, and pinch those who forget. Few of them know much about the man they celebrate or the connection between Saint Patrick's Day and Easter, but the life of Saint Patrick is actually an amazing testimony of redemption.

Saint Patrick was the missionary in the 400s who brought Christianity to Ireland. This great man, whose name is among the most revered in Irish history, was not originally from the Emerald Isle. He was born in what is now Britain, when the Roman Empire was in decline. As the Roman legions left, people were unprotected from invaders, and a band of Irish robbers kidnapped Patrick when he was a young teenager. They took him to Ireland and forced him into slavery. Patrick's father had taught him to be a Christian, but it was not until he encountered the harshness of his new life that he truly turned to God. For six long years, he prayed for escape. Finally, with help he attributed to the Lord, he ran away, walked over two hundred miles to a port, and convinced the captain of a ship to take him along when he sailed.

Patrick later studied with monks and desired only to live out the rest of his days in peace, but God had a different plan. Through a series of spiritual experiences, God called Patrick to take Christ's teachings to the untamed and violent land of his former bondage. He returned to Ireland, overcame great opposition, and was ultimately successful in introducing faith and formal education to the people. This allowed Ireland to thrive when the rest of Europe descended into what historians call the Dark Ages.[1]

Not only did Patrick see the conversion of a fierce people, but he also saw a change in himself. Patrick was transformed from a hurt, resentful, angry, and hate-filled young man into a mighty missionary who loved the Irish people so much that he chose to spend the rest of his life among them. That is redemption.

The word *redeem* means to buy back, to free from captivity, or to restore. However, it also means to change for the better.[2] When we redeem a coupon at a store, we exchange a piece of paper for something of greater value. In a similar way, Christ can exchange the worst in us for the best in Him. Because of the Atonement, not only can we be resurrected, forgiven, consoled, and healed, but we can also be improved and magnified. We can become "partakers of the divine nature" (2 Peter 1:4).

President Ezra Taft Benson declared, "Christ can change human nature."[3] However, it cannot happen against our wills. In Mosiah 15, we are warned that "the Lord redeemeth none such that rebel against him" (v. 26), not because He will not, but because He cannot. He changed water to wine (see John 2:9–10), but the water did not have to want to change. We do.

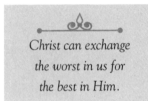

Christ can exchange the worst in us for the best in Him.

Many Christians see commandment-keeping as emerging from a changed heart. Latter-day Saints see it as part of the change process. God does not just want us to be born again but also to grow to spiritual adulthood. Only as we practice living as Christ lived, and loving as He loved, can He tutor, teach, and transform us. Grace is, as Elder Dieter F. Uchtdorf taught, "the divine assistance and endowment of strength by which we grow from the flawed and limited beings we are now into exalted beings."[4]

The title of this chapter, "Our God with Us Joining," is a phrase found within a hymn from the 1600s (*Hymns*, no. 93). It is a beautiful description of how the Lord is willing to join with us in our journey to reach our potential. We are not just making and keeping covenants *for* Him, but *with*

Him. We are not just proving ourselves *to* Him, but are improved *by* Him.

Some youth leaders took the young men and women in their ward to an escape room, where they were given a mission to accomplish. The leaders thought the youth would enjoy looking for clues and working together. Instead, the teens just sat there and did not even try. When the leaders reminded them that time was running out, one of the teens said, "They'll just let us out when the time is up. We are all going to get out anyway." Is getting out the only goal? The point of the room—and life—is not just to get out, but also to engage in the experience and help each other along the way. It is to build relationships and be a little smarter and better than when we entered. Patrick's experience in Ireland did not end with escape. God joined with him to make Patrick and the people he taught holier.

At the baptism of Christ, the sign of a dove represented the Holy Ghost. The sign was reminiscent of the dove sent out by Noah after the earth was cleansed by water. When the dove returned carrying an olive leaf (see Genesis 8:10–11), they both became symbols of hope and new life. The Holy Ghost has always served as the messenger of grace and facilitator of sanctification.[5] It is because of Him that the "old man" can become a "new man" after the image of God and Christ (Colossians 3:9–10). We may desire to stay as we are and avoid change because it is easier, but God is more interested in our growth than our comfort. We may "wish that God had designed for us a less glorious and less arduous destiny; but," as C. S. Lewis taught, "then we are wishing not for more love, but for less."[6]

> God is more interested in our growth than our comfort.

President Thomas S. Monson said, "Before Easter there must be a cross."[7] Surely, Saint Patrick did not want to be kidnapped and enslaved, but through it all, he was changed. He did not want to return to Ireland and face the very people who had hurt and abused him, but through it all, he was strengthened and magnified. The people of Ireland may not have initially desired the gospel and education Patrick offered, but through it all, they were redeemed.

Because of the Christ on Calvary, we have access to His grace "no matter where we are in the path of obedience."[8] Although it is true that no unclean thing can dwell permanently with God (see 1 Nephi 10:21), God can choose to dwell temporarily with unclean things,[9] and His influence gives us the courage to try and the strength to improve.

EASTER'S PROOFS

Christ's Witnesses Past and Present

Some people doubt that Christ was resurrected, but to believe that, they have to overlook many witnesses. There was Mary Magdalene (see John 20:16–17), as well as many other women (see Mark 16:1; Luke 8:3). There were multiple Apostles on multiple occasions (see 1 Corinthians 15:5; Luke 24; John 24) and crowds of hundreds (see 1 Corinthians 15:6), not to mention Stephen (see Acts 7:55) and Paul (see Acts 9:4–5).

Still, some could believe that these people or others who came years after them just made up those stories. That is why it is important that Christ provided additional witnesses, such as prophets in the Book of Mormon and modern prophets and temples in our day. These blessings stand as proofs of the Resurrection, but faith does not come from evidence. Evidence comes to strengthen faith. In this section, let us appreciate the fact that for believing souls, every Easter comes with "so great a cloud of witnesses" (Hebrews 12:1).

THE ROLE OF FAITH

In Ether we read, "Faith is things which are hoped for and not seen; wherefore, dispute not because ye see not, for ye receive no witness until after the trial of your faith" (Ether 12:6). The scripture does not say there is no need for evidence, but only that it must follow faith.

On our mission in Chile, two elders were teaching a man who was progressing well until they taught him about tithing. The man claimed he could never pay because he lived on a fixed income, a small pension because of his earlier military service. It was just enough to cover rent, food, and medications. When the senior companion shared the situation with his father in the United States, his dad said, "Good grief, I will pay for the man's medications the rest of his life if he will pay his tithing first."

In their next meeting, this elder begged the man to obey the commandment and promised he would receive a blessing greater than he could imagine. The missionary testified in tears that if the man would show his faith, he would never have to pay for medications again. The man declined, and the two elders left the apartment discouraged.

The junior companion said, "Why doesn't your dad just send the money first and then the guy will know he can pay his tithing without worrying?" With wisdom beyond his years, his companion said, "That's not how faith works. Without the worrying there is no faith, and without faith there is no growth." I was thankful that this missionary understood that the goal was not just to help someone pay for his medications. The goal was to help someone draw closer to God.

When the Apostle Thomas heard about the Resurrection, he said he would not believe until he saw for himself. When the Lord appeared to him, He said, "Thomas, because thou hast seen me, thou hast believed: blessed are they that have not seen, and yet have believed" (John 20:29). The Lord does not just want us to believe in Him. He also knows how important it is for us to desire to believe in Him. Elder Bruce C. Hafen taught, "The Lord has used the highly visible forms of his power so sparingly—enough to leave us with clear witnesses but not enough to compel us to believe."[1] There has to be room for doubt and belief in order to make discipleship a choice. Only then does God know where our hearts are.[2]

Demanding evidence—a sign—before faith is as futile

as trying to gain knowledge before humility, skill before practice, and strength of character before self-discipline. The goal is not just to see Christ, but to be more like Him when we do. Elder Dieter F. Uchtdorf spoke at Brigham Young University and stated, "If you want something of true and lasting value, something of eternal significance, something that connects the now with the eternities, patience and diligence are required. . . . Perhaps the Lord wants us to prove to Him—or to ourselves—just how sincerely we want the truth. Maybe the effort He requires is how we learn to value the truth. Maybe that is how we prepare ourselves to receive and accept the truth."[3]

> *There has to be room for doubt and belief in order to make discipleship a choice. Only then does God know where our hearts are.*

Alma taught, "Yea, there are many who do say: If thou wilt show unto us a sign from heaven, then we shall know of a surety; then we shall believe" (Alma 32:17). Alma then explained, "Faith is not to have a perfect knowledge of things" (v. 21). In my mind, I picture a gas tank that can be full (perfect knowledge) or empty (complete faithlessness), but most of us are somewhere between those two extremes. Our faith is at a quarter tank or half tank and we have to continually keep refilling by hoping "for things which are not seen, which are true" (v. 21).

Some define integrity as aligning our behavior with our beliefs, but children align their behavior with their beliefs each time they place lost teeth beneath their pillows or write letters to the North Pole. True integrity is aligning our beliefs and behavior with truth.[4] But how do we know belief in Christ and God is not in the same category as belief in the tooth fairy?

Jesus said we could judge truth by its fruits (see Matthew 7:16). As children grow, the fruits of childhood fantasies like the tooth fairy fade, while the fruits of faith in God expand, multiply, and grow ever sweeter. So, is it wrong for parents to lend a hand to the tooth fairy and Easter bunny? Do we do a disservice to children when we read stories about fairy godmothers and magic lamps? Not according to children's literature experts, who say that such things prepare believing hearts. They instill positive attitudes and the hope that good can triumph over evil, people can change, and love can endure.[5] From a spiritual perspective, such things can make it easier for children to develop faith in God.

> *True integrity is aligning our beliefs and behavior with truth.*

Alma said, "If ye will awake and arouse your faculties, even to an experiment upon my words, and exercise a particle of faith, yea, even if ye can no more than desire to believe, let this desire work in you, even until ye . . . can give place for a portion of my words" (Alma 32:27). Elder Uchtdorf explained, "Now some of you might say, 'In order to have greater belief in God, I have to believe? But that is exactly my problem. What if I can't believe?' The answer is: Then hope and desire to believe. . . . To desire to believe does not mean to pretend. It means to open your heart to the possibility of spiritual things, to lay aside skepticism and cynicism."[6] In other words, put a little gas in the tank and see if the car moves. The gas just has to come first.

Alma challenged his listeners to plant the word like a seed in their hearts. "If it be a true seed, . . . it will begin to swell within your breasts; and when you feel these swelling motions, ye will begin to say within yourselves—It must needs be that this is a good seed, . . . for it beginneth to enlarge my soul; yea, it beginneth to enlighten my understanding, yea, it beginneth to be delicious to me" (Alma 32:28). Alma then asked, "O then, is not this real?" (v. 35).

Because of the Christ on Calvary, we have the freedom to choose. No one is forced to believe. When we choose faith in Christ, multiple witnesses and evidences assure us we are not wrong. Because of the Christ on Calvary, as our faith grows, we grow. The fruits are real and, as Alma put it, delicious.

ANOTHER TESTAMENT

*A*nother testament? Why *another* testament? Jesus has the Bible. That's testament enough." The words came from a man speaking to my parents while they were on their mission in Macon, Georgia. They had just offered him a copy of the Book of Mormon.

My dad asked him, "How many Christian churches are there?"

The man responded, "Maybe two or three hundred. Perhaps even as many as four hundred."

"In actuality," said my dad, "the *World Christian Encyclopedia* says there are over 33,000[1]—thousands of Christian denominations all testifying of Christ in thousands of different ways, all interpreting the same Bible and doctrine in thousands of different ways. Another testament of Christ can verify and clarify the Bible." The man had never thought of it like that before and accepted the book.

The Book of Mormon is not here to displace the Bible

but can be a welcome additional witness of the truths contained therein and offer more light. For example, in the Bible we never see the phrase *plan of salvation*, but in the Book of Mormon, we see it multiple times (see, for example, Jarom 1:2; Alma 24:14; 42:5). The Bible teaches about the Fall of Adam and Eve, but in the Book of Mormon we learn that it was positive rather than negative (see 2 Nephi 19–25). In the Bible we learn about Christ's Atonement, but in the Book of Mormon we learn it was "prepared from the foundation of the world" (Mosiah 4:6). The Bible speaks of resurrection and forgiveness, but the Book of Mormon speaks about additional blessings that flow from the Atonement of Christ (see Alma 7:12). In the Bible, baptism is presented only as a cleansing, but in the Book of Mormon we learn it is a covenant (see Mosiah 18:10). The Bible invites people to come to Christ, but the Book of Mormon invites people to Christ by covenant (see Book of Mormon title page).

The Book of Mormon has power because of its contents, but also because of how it came forth in our day. The Bible came to us through the sacrifice of many people over many centuries, as did the Book of Mormon, but an angel delivered the actual record of the latter. Many scholars translated the Bible over years. People could argue that the text we have today is a result of scholarship with little involvement from God. Such is not the case for the Book of Mormon.

Joseph Smith, a young man with little formal education, translated the Book of Mormon in roughly sixty days. It could *not* have happened without God's involvement.

Although some people may wish for a more academic or reasonable explanation of finding and translating the plates, they do not realize that such an explanation would weaken rather than strengthen the book's impact. Consider the Dead Sea Scrolls. A shepherd boy discovered them in 1947. He saw no angel who led him to the scrolls. Rather, he stumbled upon the cave where they lay hidden. Some of the most knowledgeable and respected scholars of our time translated them. In fact, professors at Brigham Young University were enormously helpful in the translation and preservation of those ancient records. Today you can visit a museum in Jerusalem and see some of the original scrolls.

The story of the discovery and translation of the Dead Sea Scrolls is reasonable and acceptable. Unlike the Book of Mormon, the Dead Sea Scrolls have caused little controversy and have never been the focus of any Broadway musical. That said, they have also had little spiritual impact. I do not mean to disrespect the amazing find or the fascinating contents of the scrolls. Historically, it was a discovery of great significance. However, I have yet to meet or even hear about one person who stopped smoking, saved a marriage, chose to be baptized, or attended the temple because of the Dead Sea Scrolls.

Conversely, the Book of Mormon is inseparable from stories of angels, golden plates, interpreters, seer stones, and even the appearance of God and Jesus. Were it just a book filled with the teachings of ancient prophets, it may not be any more valuable to people than the Dead Sea Scrolls. It is also the story of how the Book of Mormon came forth that has kindled and validated the faith of millions.

When speaking about the coming forth of the Book of Mormon, Mildred Eyring, mother of President Henry B. Eyring, concluded that an explanation can be "logical even though it appears to be miraculous. The explanation that Joseph Smith gave is the best one that has been given."[2] Joseph's explanation of how the book came to be requires us to acknowledge God's involvement in the creation, preservation, and translation of the record. It stands as stunning proof that God is real and involved in our lives today.

We are all free to accept or reject these remarkable truths, but either way, we have to take a side. We cannot apathetically brush the Book of Mormon aside like the Dead Sea Scrolls. Those who reject it do so at their own peril (see 2 Nephi 33:14; 3 Nephi 21:11). Those who accept it will be grateful.

When my son Russell served his mission in Spain, he and his companion moved into a room of an apartment owned by Adela, an eighty-year-old grandmother. Although not a member of the Church, she showed the missionaries a copy of the Book of Mormon that another set of missionaries had left when they had rented from her years earlier. Russell and his companion began to teach Adela more about the book. When they came home for lunch, they would often find her reading it. She took notes and asked them many questions. As her testimony grew, she began attending Sunday meetings and decided to be baptized.

Adela joined the Church in November of 2005—the same year President Gordon B. Hinckley issued a challenge to the Saints to read the Book of Mormon before the end of the year. After Adela's baptism, Russell told her of the prophet's invitation and the blessings awaiting those who accepted it. During the Christmas holidays, she went to her daughter's house to spend the vacation with family. However, she had not quite finished reading the Book of Mormon. On New Year's Eve, she asked her daughter to take her home early so she could finish the book before midnight. The next day this white-haired sister grabbed my son with both arms and said, "Thank you for coming into my life and for bringing this book to me."

Because of the Christ on Calvary, we have the blessings of the Atonement. Because of the Book of Mormon, we have evidence we can hold in our hands that Christ and the blessings of His Atonement are real and within our reach.

MODERN PROPHETS' WITNESSES OF CHRIST

Y ou're from Utah? Are you a member of that church?"
Although I have been asked those questions many
times on flights bound for Salt Lake City, this time the conversation was happening between two men sitting in the
seats behind me and I was only listening.

The man answered, "No, I'm not, but I know lots of
people who are."

The other man asked, "So, what are they like?"

"They are the greatest people ever. Seriously, I have
never met people who are more kind and generous, but they
sure have a lot of weird beliefs that are just plain wrong."

Did this man realize how contradictory his statement
was? How can "weird beliefs that are just plain wrong" yield
"the greatest people ever"? How can good fruit come from
a bad tree?

The conversation continued: "So how did their church
start?"

"Joseph Smith started it."

"Who was he?"

"Just some guy who started another church. He doesn't really matter."

That was the end of their little chat about the Church of Jesus Christ, and they quickly moved on to sports—a subject about which both were much better informed. I was no longer listening, but I could not get the one man's final comment out of my head: Joseph Smith was just some guy who started another church.

Obviously, this man was totally unaware of how John Taylor felt about the Prophet: "Joseph Smith, the Prophet and Seer of the Lord, has done more, save Jesus only, for the salvation of men in this world, than any other man that ever lived in it" (D&C 135:3). That does not sound like "just some guy" to me.

Many who are not members of the Church also recognize Joseph Smith's contributions. Obviously, the man on the plane was not aware that *Smithsonian* magazine has included Joseph Smith in their listing of "the 100 most significant Americans of all time" and in the category of Religious Figures, Joseph Smith was number one.[1] It certainly seems like the man on the plane was shortsighted to say Joseph Smith "doesn't really matter."

I wish the man sitting behind me on the plane had been sitting next to me. He would have gotten a very different answer. I would have said, "Jesus Christ has never had a more faithful witness than Joseph Smith. Everything I hold most dear about my Savior is thanks to Joseph Smith."

Joseph Smith was a witness of Jesus Christ. Because of his testimony and teachings, we see Christ clearly. But what if Joseph Smith lied? What if he made it all up? Such questions are important to ask in a world full of frauds, con artists, and manipulators. Here are only a few of many reasons I trust the Prophet.

First, his family believed him. Family members are often the ones who know us best. Sometimes I ask my students, "If your family were to play a game tomorrow, how many of you know exactly who would be most likely to cheat?" All the hands go up. Joseph Smith's family was no different. They knew each other well. The fact that they believed Joseph and made great sacrifices to follow him says a lot to me.

> *Joseph Smith was a witness of Jesus Christ. Because of his testimony and teachings, we see Christ clearly.*

Second, there is no sequel to the Book of Mormon. If Joseph were some storytelling genius like George Lucas, who invented Star Wars, or J. K. Rowling, who gave us Harry Potter, why didn't he produce additional volumes of the story as they both did? The Book of Mormon speaks of records to come forth from other groups of Israelites. If Joseph

Smith were such a capable author, why didn't he "bring forth" those records as well? Why wasn't he driven by the same motives that seem to push other authors?

Third, Joseph delegated authority. I have had enough micromanaging leaders in my life to know that people cling to authority. However, it seems Joseph Smith could not delegate fast enough. He called others and did not just assign them tasks to do, but gave them authority and autonomy. He expected them to seek their own direction from heaven, make their decisions, and be accountable for them. The fact that the Prophet trusted so many helps me trust him.

Fourth, Joseph Smith's revelations were never self-serving. He claimed revelation from the Lord, but he was open and honest about what it contained. There were times when the Lord reprimanded him, and he published those rebukes for all to see. It seems to me that if Joseph Smith were inventing his heavenly communications, they would have had nothing but positive things to say about him.

Finally, Joseph Smith died for what he believed. There is no deeper evidence of commitment. I remember when I taught sixth grade before teaching at Brigham Young University and my students and I would work difficult math problems together. When we finally arrived at the answer, I would say, "Are you sure that's correct?"

All the students would respond, "Yes!"

I would then ask, "Will you stake your recess on it?"

Suddenly everyone would be quiet. Joseph Smith was willing to stake much more than his recess on the answers he received from God. He gave his life for them. Before he and his brother Hyrum went to Carthage, they had escaped across the Mississippi River. However, when friends asked them to return, they did so, knowing all the while they would be, as Joseph put it, "butchered." The Prophet said, "I am going like a lamb to the slaughter, but I am calm as a summer's morning. I have a conscience void of offense towards God and towards all men."[2] Considering the gravity of his situation, those do not sound like the words of a con artist or liar to me.

Joseph Smith was the first in an unbroken line of modern prophets and apostles who have come after him. Anciently, Peter selected Matthias to fill the vacancy left in the quorum by Judas (see Acts 1:25–26). When other Apostles were killed, like James (see Acts 12:1–2), more Apostles, such as Paul, were chosen (see Acts 14:14). In the Rome Italy Temple Visitors' Center there are replicas of Thorvaldsen's statues of Christ and His original Apostles. Visitors quickly notice that the artist sculpted Paul in place of Judas. By so doing, he recognized that Apostles were meant to be replaced. Imagine what he would have thought when early in 2019, all the living Apostles gathered in Rome and stood in front of his statues for a special photograph.

When our family lived in Chile, we had the opportunity of serving at the same time that Elder Jeffrey R. Holland was also living there and directing the work in that country. He and Sister Holland knew from personal experience how hard it can be for kids to move, so they always gave our children a little extra attention and kindness.

One day, Whitney, our seventh-grader, came home from school and announced, "Elder Holland is in my math book." She then showed me a problem that read: "Yesterday it took Jeff Holland 1 hour to get to work. This morning, Jeff drove to the train station in 20 minutes, waited for the train for 7 minutes, rode the train for 12 minutes, and then walked for 15 minutes to get to work. How long did it take Jeff to get to work this morning?"

I thought it was funny, so I photocopied the page and attached a sticky note that said, "Elder Holland, could you please help Whitney with her homework?"

A few days later, an envelope arrived from Elder Holland's office with a handwritten message inside: "Dear Whitney, I was pleased you discovered my day job. I regularly submit math problems for textbooks and sometimes I just don't know whose name to use. I think I will use yours next. (If Whitney Wilcox has 5 boyfriends in Provo and gains 1 a day for 14 days in Chile, how many of them will be baptized, go on missions, and want to marry her?) Thanks for being here! I am immensely proud of you! Jeff Holland."

That little note has become a family treasure—not just because it was funny, but because it helped strengthen a seventh-grader's testimony of the reality of living apostles and prophets. The letter demonstrated validation and love that Whitney recognized as attributes of the Savior. It was not hard for Whitney to connect the dots between Elder Holland and the Lord He represents.

Living witnesses of Christ matter. Not only do we receive the Lord's direction through them, but their testimonies become an additional layer in the foundation of our testimonies of the Savior (see 1 Corinthians 3:10–11).

Their witnesses of God strengthen our witnesses. Their testimonies of Christ fortify our testimonies. They are not pretending. They would not dedicate their lives to a fairy tale.[3]

Because of the Christ on Calvary, all men and women can know that God is our Heavenly Father and He loves us. Because of the Christ on Calvary, we can one day feel His embrace. Because Christ lives today, He can lead us through special witnesses who call to us, "We're with you!"[4] Because of the Christ and His modern prophets, we are never alone.

> *Living witnesses of Christ matter. Their testimonies of Christ fortify our testimonies.*

INFALLIBLE PROOFS

After His Resurrection, Jesus ministered to His followers for forty days. In Acts 1:3 we read that they received "many infallible proofs." Those words leave readers wondering, "What infallible proofs did they need if they were already with the resurrected Christ?" The Greek word that was translated as "infallible proofs" is *tekmeriois*, which means "sure signs or tokens."[1] Those early Saints did not need proof of Christ's Resurrection, but they still needed what Luke called the "promise of the Father" (Acts 1:4), or as Elder Bruce R. McConkie taught, the endowment.[2]

We receive the same infallible proofs in temples today. Along with prophets throughout every dispensation, temples are witnesses of Easter. As Paul reasoned, if Jesus did not rise again and there is no life after death, why would we do vicarious ordinances for the departed? (see 1 Corinthians 15:29). Each temple is evidence of the testimonies of millions of members who sacrifice to build, staff, and serve within them. Together we sing, "[We] know that [our] Redeemer lives." He is our "Prophet, Priest, and King" (*Hymns*, no. 136).

A prophet sees "afar off" (Moses 6:27) and shares his vision with others. A priest officiates in saving ordinances, and a king is one who owns and presides. His is the responsibility to protect and provide for those who depend upon him.[3] In the temple, we not only learn how Christ fulfills each of these roles in our lives, but also how, by means of His Atonement, He intends to make us prophets and prophetesses, priests and priestesses, kings and queens.

On June 2, 1953, Queen Elizabeth II's coronation was televised. For the first time in history, people from around the world were able to observe the thousand-year-old ritual. The book *The Crown Jewels* explains how the coronation is imbued with meaning from Biblical antiquity.[4] The monarch makes an oath, "swearing to govern faithfully with justice and mercy, to uphold the Gospel, and to maintain the doctrine and worship of the Church."[5] He or she is then anointed with holy oil. This is followed by the investiture of power, knowledge, wisdom, and majesty from on high, during which the monarch dresses in special robes and receives a series of religious objects or tokens one at a time before an altar. In the official photo taken of Queen Elizabeth on her coronation day, she held a scepter in her right hand and an orb in her cupped left hand.

The robes are "based on" or "inspired" by the robes worn by ancient high priests and include a simple linen undergarment, a tunic or mantle, a priestly stole embroidered with "symbolic plants," and a head covering.[6] Queen Elizabeth wore only a crown, but kings before her wore a crown atop a cloth cap, and queens, such as Queen Victoria, wore a crown atop a veil covering their hair and shoulders.[7]

The chair used during Queen Elizabeth's coronation is the same chair that has been used for over seven hundred years. It was made to enclose the Stone of Destiny. Tradition claims this stone was brought from the Holy Land and was the very stone upon which Jacob once slept. Modern research has failed to show a connection between the stone currently housed in the Castle of Edinburgh in Scotland and stones in the Holy Land, but it is fascinating that so many kings and queens have claimed authority from sitting atop a stone that was supposedly touched by an ancient prophet.

What did Joseph Smith know of coronation rituals when the endowment was revealed to him? Similarities seem to indicate that both experiences have shared ancient roots. One has been passed down and altered through years of apostasy. The other was revealed in our day as part of the Restoration of all things. Both assert connections with Biblical antiquity, but while royalty and religious leaders on the one hand honor a stone supposedly touched by an ancient prophet, Joseph Smith spoke of receiving authority directly from ancient prophets. The endowment was revealed to teach us how to one day return to God's presence, and in the temple we do work for the dead, but these experiences also provide helpful perspective as we deal with life's struggles here and now.

When I was a boy, I faced rejection from my peers. I spent childhood years in Africa where there was little emphasis on sports. Our family moved back to Utah just before I turned eight, and suddenly I found myself in a world where sports seemed to mean everything. Children at my school realized quickly I did not know much about sports and quit picking me for their teams because they did not want to lose on my account. I quit volunteering to play because I did not want them to lose on my account either. My dad and brothers tried to catch me up, but I was not motivated to practice something I did not do well. By middle school, I was at the bottom of the social food chain and the target of ridicule and bullying.

It is a little embarrassing to write about it now, but one of my coping mechanisms was to make believe I was a king who had been placed in hiding for my protection. People did not know my real identity so they treated me as if I were nothing, but deep inside I knew I was a king, and someday they would know it too. I do not know where the story line came from. Perhaps the idea first came from a book or a movie, but whatever the source, my private role-playing got me through some difficult days. When I was especially low, I pictured myself in a palace dressed in royal robes watching the surprised looks on the faces of my peers when they finally discovered my true identity.

I never shared this imaginary world with anyone. People already had plenty to tease me about without knowing about my pretending. The reason I share it now is that, as strange as it may seem, it prepared me for the temple. Before I went for the first time, my parents and leaders told me a little of what to expect, but no one told me that I would be living out my childhood fantasy. There I was in a palace! There I was being anointed and dressed in royal robes! There I was surrounded by family members and friends and feeling their love and acceptance. I felt valued and important. I felt royal.

In the temple, we step away from the world and are reminded of our true identities and potential. We are princes and princesses, sons and daughters of a King and Queen who live in "royal courts on high" (*Hymns*, no. 292). We are learning to become like Them. Surely, Adam and Eve needed that perspective when they felt like failures. The early members of the Church we read about in Acts needed that same perspective. The infallible proofs—signs and tokens—they received were not just a witness *of* Christ, but also a validation of their worth *from* Christ. The same infallible proofs helped Saints in Joseph Smith's day. They were at the bottom of the social food chain, facing ridicule and rejection. They knew they were God's chosen people, but no one treated them that way. They needed their endowments in Nauvoo to help them keep perspective and gather courage. They needed to enter God's palace and be reminded of their identities. They needed to feel royal.

We need the same strength and vision today to help us endure. We all face unfairness, judgment, and rejection. In such moments, we do not need to pretend we are kings and queens in hiding. Instead, we can *know* we are kings and queens in training. President John Taylor said, "You are aiming to become kings and priests to the Lord, and queens and priestesses to him."[8] The temple teaches us that my childhood escape is actually a reality. I once wrote a poem to remind myself of this truth and still recite it each time I drive to the temple:

God's Palace

I go to the temple to pray with my brothers.
Princes all are we, preparing for eternity.
I go to the temple to be with my sisters.
Princesses all, preparing to heed the King's call.
The temple, the temple,
House of beauty, house of prayer.

The temple is God's palace.
I feel His royal Spirit there.

I go to the temple to learn of my Savior.
Symbols of His love, revealing truth from up above.
I go to the temple to learn my potential.
God's hand in mine teaches of His grace divine.
The temple, the temple,
House of beauty, house of prayer.
The temple is God's palace.
I feel His royal Spirit there.

Because of the Christ on Calvary, we have the promise of new life, and because of the "promise of the Father" (Acts 1:4), the endowment shared within temples, we can return to God's presence. The Savior has provided many special witnesses of His role and reality, but also "infallible proofs" (Acts 1:3) of our worth and potential. Because of Christ, we can enter God's palace, be anointed, be dressed in special robes, and receive divine help from our Prophet, Priest, and King as we strive to become more like Him.

EASTER'S PROMISES

The Blessings of Worship and Discipleship

Some books are not as good as the covers make them appear. Some movies are not as good as their trailers. The attitudes of some professional athletes and musicians often spoil games and concerts. There is a lot of hype and letdown in the world. Sadly, we are sometimes let down in more important and complex matters as well, such as education, marriage, children, and employment. However, for me, one thing that has definitely lived up to all the hype is the fullness of truth contained in the restored gospel. Christ and His Atonement have always surpassed my greatest expectations and filled me with hope. The promises of Easter breathe life into my worship and discipleship.

These promises include the eternal perspective that helps us deal with trials. They also include sharing that blessing with others through missionary work and ministering to those who wander. But, ultimately, the greatest promise of Easter is fulfilled as we truly internalize and appreciate the suffering of Christ and the covenant relationship we have with Him.

DISAPPOINTED WITH GOD

Broken homes, lost jobs, shattered dreams, poor health, failed romances—amid these traumas and more, even faithful believers begin to wonder if God cares. "If He does," they reason, "why doesn't He reach down and just fix all this?" In his book *Disappointment with God*,[1] Christian author Philip Yancey has pointed out that too often when something goes wrong we feel betrayed, as if we have kept our end of the bargain while God has failed to keep His. We look up toward heaven, shake a fist, and yell, "After all I have done for you, this is what I get?"[2] The author explained that behind the pain and loss felt in such moments, there are three larger questions. "Few people ask them aloud, for they seem at best impolite, at worst heretical."[3] Nevertheless, they are there, demanding answers: "Is God unfair? . . . Is God silent? . . . Is God hidden?"[4]

"Is God unfair? Why doesn't he consistently punish evil people and reward good people? Why do awful things happen to

people good and bad, with no discernible pattern?"[5] Although it is true that bad things sometimes happen to good people, let us not forget that good things happen to good people, too. Still, without an eternal perspective, who are we to decide what is good or bad? There have been times in my life when something I thought was bad turned out to be good.

Sometimes we confuse God with Santa. We picture Him dishing out coal or candy depending on whether we have been naughty or nice. Greater understanding comes when we see God as He truly is—a loving Father who is teaching us and, as we turn to Him, making all things work together for our good (see Romans 8:28; D&C 105:40).

Paul taught that sometimes our troubles come as consequences of our own poor choices. We yoke ourselves with "unbelievers" and touch "the unclean thing" even when we have been commanded not to (2 Corinthians 6:14, 17). Paul also taught that we suffer the consequences of others' poor choices. He was beaten, stoned, robbed, and left "in cold and nakedness" (2 Corinthians 11:25, 27). In addition, Paul attributed some of our trials to simply living in mortality. He lamented about "a thorn in the flesh" that bothered him even after he had prayed multiple times that it be taken away (2 Corinthians 12:7–8). Based on Paul's comments elsewhere in his epistles, Bible scholars have suggested that his thorn may have been a degenerative eye disease.[6]

Whatever the source of his struggles and ours, Paul

wrote, "We are troubled on every side, yet not distressed; we are perplexed, but not in despair; persecuted, but not forsaken; cast down, but not destroyed" (2 Corinthians 4:8–9). Such peace is possible because of the bigger picture provided by the plan of salvation. As psychiatrist and author Theodore Isaac Rubin wrote, "The problem is not that there are problems. The problem is expecting otherwise and thinking that having problems is a problem."[7] Earth life is not a vacation but a school where we are learning to become more like the Lord.

Elder Neal A. Maxwell wrote, "How can you and I really expect to glide naively through life, as if to say, 'Lord, give me experience, but not grief, not sorrow, not pain, not opposition, not betrayal, and certainly not to be forsaken. Keep from me, Lord, all those experiences, which made Thee what Thou art! Then, let me come and dwell with Thee and fully share Thy joy!'"[8]

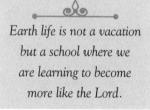

Earth life is not a vacation but a school where we are learning to become more like the Lord.

God may seem unfair when we consider how some are born to privilege and others have nothing. Some have health, while others suffer with lifelong mental and physical illnesses. Some have the gospel and others not. The plan of salvation assures that mortality is not the beginning or the end. It is only one more step in a long-term, individualized education plan that has as its ultimate goal, as Paul stated, "even your perfection" (2 Corinthians 13:9). We must trust that no differences in circumstances need to keep us from learning the personalized lessons God has for us. Elder Jeffrey R. Holland assured, "Pain in this world is *not* evidence that God doesn't love [us]."[9] Rather, because God has promised to "consecrate [our] afflictions for [our] gain" (2 Nephi 2:2), it can actually be seen as evidence that He does.[10]

Elder Bruce C. Hafen and Marie K. Hafen have written, "To snatch us completely out of life's unfairness and injustices . . . would negate the very reason we came to earth, which is to master the traits of godliness even while under intense pressure. His grace allows us to be healed from and sanctified by that pressure without being crushed by it."[11]

> *No differences in circumstances need to keep us from learning the personalized lessons God has for us.*

"*Is God silent? If he is so concerned about our doing his will, why doesn't he reveal that will more plainly?*"[12] Although it is true that we do not always get step-by-step instructions and immediate answers from God, let's not forget the times when we do. Still, with our limited perspective, who are we to decide just how much direction we need? Many times, I have ended up thanking God for *not* answering my earlier prayers.

Sometimes we confuse God with a rich uncle. We picture Him dishing out sage advice and spoiling us by granting our every desire. Greater understanding comes when we see God as He truly is—a loving Father who is teaching us and who does all things for our good whether or not we like it. God is not interested in what will make Him popular. He is concerned only with what is best. He does not do "anything save it be for the benefit of the world; for he loveth the world" (2 Nephi 26:24).

One research study examined babies' sleep habits. Some babies were allowed to stay up as late as they wanted until they fell asleep naturally. Others were put to bed at a set time, but picked up and comforted the moment they cried. A third group was put to bed at a set time and allowed to cry for a few minutes before being checked on. If the crying continued, the time between check-ins was gradually increased as long as everything was found to be okay. Results showed that not only did the babies in the third group sleep longer, but they fell back to sleep faster than the other groups after waking up in the middle of the night.[13] Another study examined how babies learn to walk. Parents who allowed their little ones to fall saw them progress twice as fast as the children of parents who hovered over every step and prevented every tumble.[14]

Both these studies help explain why God, the perfect parent, is sometimes slow to direct our every move and come running the minute we call. He has given us prophets "to guide us in these latter days" (*Hymns*, no. 19) and other leaders at every level of Church organization. We also receive guidance from parents and the Spirit. Nevertheless, we were sent to earth to obtain experience and develop faith. That purpose would be frustrated if God gave personal direction immediately for every decision and individual circumstance. Elder Richard G. Scott taught, "When we explain a problem and proposed solution [to Heavenly Father], sometimes He answers yes, sometimes no. Often He withholds an answer, not for lack of concern, but because He loves us—perfectly. He wants us to apply truths He has given us. For us to grow, we need to trust our ability to make correct decisions."[15]

For me, sometimes answers to prayer have come in such stunningly direct ways that I marvel. Other times God withholds direction and answers. On those occasions, I do not see His silence as evidence that He is too busy or does not care. Instead, I see it as evidence that He trusts me. He knows I have made correct decisions in the past, and He trusts me to do it again.

"Is God hidden? Why doesn't he simply show up sometime, visibly, and dumbfound the sceptics once and for all?"[16] Although it is true that God, Christ, and angels do not show up regularly, let's not forget the times they do. Scriptures are full of testimonies of those who have seen them. The history

of the Restoration is full of manifestations. Many members of the Church today have experiences that are too sacred to share casually. Still, with our limited perspective, who are we to decide when God should or should not show up? Does He exist solely to satisfy our curiosity and quiet critics?

Sometimes we confuse God with a butler. We picture Him coming when summoned in order to attend to our every whim and impress our friends. Greater understanding comes when we see God as He truly is—a loving Father who is teaching us and who sent us here to "walk by faith, not by sight" (2 Corinthians 5:7). Anyone can choose the right when being supervised. If a parent, teacher, or boss is watching, even slackers can act as if they are doing their best. The key is to be making those choices even when no one is looking. Imagine the joy Heavenly Father feels when He can say of us what Paul said of the Philippian Saints, "Wherefore, my beloved, . . . ye have always obeyed, not . . . in my presence only, but . . . in my absence" (Philippians 2:12).

In the Book of Mormon, we read about Aaron being confronted by an Amalekite who asked, "Hast thou seen an angel? Why do not angels appear unto us? Behold are not this people as good as thy people?" (Alma 21:5). This question was asked in an argumentative and antagonistic way, but I have heard the same question from young people who genuinely and humbly wonder why they have not seen God, Christ, and angels.

Perhaps they think such an experience would automatically strengthen their faith, but divine manifestations did not strengthen the testimonies of Laman and Lemuel. Maybe these young people think that seeing an angel would finally motivate them to break their bad habits, but heavenly visitations do not guarantee change. The Savior said that those who reject the testimony of scripture and prophets would probably reject the testimony of angels were they to appear to them (see Luke 16:31). Maybe these young people think that an angel would be a sure sign of God's love and approval. However, God's love is not measured by visitations. In fact, not seeing manifestations may also be evidence of His love. In Alma 32:19 we read, "More cursed is he that knoweth the will of God and doeth it not, than he that only believeth . . . and falleth into transgression."

Most of us do not have visitations for the same reason we do not give young children keys to the car. The kids may want them and even beg for them, but we know they are not yet ready for the responsibility that comes with them.[17]

President Boyd K. Packer spoke of a spiritual manifestation he received and said, "Such an experience is at once a light to follow and a burden to carry."[18] No wonder we are told in Doctrine and Covenants 67:13–14, "Ye are not able to abide the presence of God now, neither the ministering of angels; wherefore, continue in patience until ye are perfected. . . . In mine own due time, ye shall see and know."

When people question, "Is God unfair, silent, and hidden?" the joyful answer Latter-day Saints share is that He is not! God is anxious to bless us. God speaks to us through prophets in our day and directs us through personal revelation. He is anxious to communicate with us and reveal Himself. When He seems to be doing otherwise, we can find answers within the broader perspective provided by the plan of salvation.

Because of the Christ on Calvary, we never have to be disappointed with God for long. There are answers to our questions—even the ones we do not always ask aloud. Because of the Christ on Calvary, "trials make our faith grow stronger" (*Hymns*, no. 280). Because of the Christ on Calvary, the veil between man and God was "rent in twain from the top to the bottom" (Mark 15:38). Where once only one high priest could pass through the veil, now we all will have that opportunity. God is no longer out of reach. Christ reveals His "secret unto his servants the prophets" (Amos 3:7) and to all who "ask in faith, nothing wavering" (James 1:6). God and Christ can and will manifest themselves to us "in word, and also in power, in very deed" (1 Nephi 14:1).

SEARCH AND RESCUE

When it came to Easter egg hunts, my brothers, cousins, and I were pros. We had rules about how long the hiders could take and exactly how much of each egg had to be showing. There were boundaries we could not cross and limits as to how many eggs could be hidden in the same place. That restriction came into being the year I hid all the eggs in the rain gutter. Inevitably in every hunt, more eggs were hidden than found. One or two always got lost and would not turn up until later in the summer when we were weeding a flowerbed or working in the garden.

One year, so many eggs went missing that my mom sent my younger brother Chris and me on what she called a search-and-rescue mission. She had planned on using those eggs in her potato salad, so luckily we found enough to save the day. God sends us on a similar search-and-rescue mission—only the stakes are much higher. This time we are finding His children.

After Christ's Resurrection, one of the first things He told His disciples was, "Go ye into all the world, and preach the gospel to every creature. He that believeth and is baptized shall be saved" (Mark 16:15–16). Can anyone truly celebrate Easter without being filled with a desire to follow that commission? Of course, finding our sisters and brothers is much more difficult than finding Easter eggs, because people move around and sometimes go to great lengths to remain hidden.

It would be wonderful if they told us where they were, but even when they do not, God knows where they are and when it is the right time for them. As we team up with Him to search out and rescue our brothers and sisters, amazing things can happen.

Once a young teenage boy went into a grove of trees. No, we are not talking about Joseph Smith in upstate New York, but Ryan London in Michigan. Ryan was not looking for a church to join. He grew up in a close-knit Catholic family that attended mass, observed Advent and Lent, and prayed the rosary. His mom even had Ryan practice his handwriting by copying psalms from the Bible. Prayers were memorized, but they were still satisfying and meaningful to him.

The family lived on ten acres, half of which were wooded, and Ryan liked playing in the trees. One morning as he heard the leaves rustling in the wind and saw sunlight streaking through the branches and lighting patches of ground beneath his feet, Ryan realized the beauty of nature surrounding him could not have happened by chance. The wind, trees, and sunlight witnessed to him there is a God.

Ryan's first encounter with the Church of Jesus Christ was through a TV documentary. He was interested, even though it sounded a little strange to him. He recognized the doctrinal holes in his Catholic faith but still had yet to study another religion that made more sense to him. Not long after, Ryan met a Latter-day Saint in a Facebook group and started asking her questions. She sent him a copy of the Book of Mormon.

Ryan began reading but got bogged down at the point when Nephi started including the sermons of his father and brother along with the writings of Isaiah. Nephi called these "the more sacred things" (1 Nephi 19:5), but no matter how "plain and precious" (v. 3) Nephi thought they were, Ryan was not ready for them yet and shelved the book.

Several years later he met another Latter-day Saint on Facebook named Silvia. Silvia had grown up in Oaxaca, Mexico. Like Ryan, she had been Catholic, but her family had never practiced. When Silvia was fourteen, some Latter-day Saint elders rented a room from her neighbor. They kicked a soccer ball around in the street with Silvia's older brother when they were coming and going and one day asked to meet his family. Silvia's mom did not want to listen, but she gave the elders permission to teach her children. Silvia remembers attending church services in a rented house and being surprised when she encountered some of her friends from school there. She always knew those friends were different in a good way, and now she knew why. She felt something special in sacrament meeting.

Silvia enjoyed the missionaries' lessons, but she had just gone through a similar process with people from the Catholic church, preparing her for her first Communion. She was confused and did not know what to believe. Soon the elders were transferred out of the area and sisters arrived. They did not know the elders had been teaching Silvia and her siblings. Her brother and sister were fine with not continuing, but Silvia missed the feeling she'd had at sacrament meeting, and after a few months she sought out the sisters and asked if they would teach her. Silvia was baptized, served a mission in Mexico City, and moved to Utah. She had graduated from Brigham Young University and was working when Ryan started communicating with her online. Before long, phone calls replaced online chats and their relationship blossomed.

Like the carefully hidden Easter eggs, one young woman had been hidden in Mexico, but some missionaries found her. Now she was helping to find another person hidden in Michigan. Ryan and Silvia determined to meet. Ryan traveled to Utah, and Silvia took him to the open house of the recently remodeled Ogden Temple. The next day, Saturday, they visited Temple Square in Salt Lake City and then walked down the street to the Catholic Cathedral of the Madeleine and attended the Saturday evening mass. Despite the differences in their faiths, the more time they spent together, the more they felt like the puzzle pieces fit. They were married and settled in Provo.

That is where I met them. They attended my ward, and I helped care for their son Benny in nursery on Sundays. I had no idea Ryan was not a member. The missionaries had tried to teach him a few years earlier but found themselves unable to answer Ryan's questions. Nothing ever came of it until Elder Wheeler and Elder Menjivar showed up and found notes about Ryan in their area record. They paid him a visit and offered to bring someone from the ward who could help answer his questions. Ryan agreed, and the elders enlisted me. Of course, I jumped at the chance.

I was pleasantly surprised that Ryan's questions were not the typical questions that emerge when people read anti-Mormon material. Rather, these sincere questions had come from Ryan's own studying, pondering, and discussions with his wife. We spoke about our premortal existence and the spirit world. We talked about degrees of glory and the ultimate destiny of mankind. Ryan asked questions about apostasy and restoration. At the end of the lesson, he agreed to another appointment.

Ryan loved going to the mountains near Provo to enjoy nature. It was in the woods of Michigan that God had first communicated His existence to him. Now, it was in trees in Provo Canyon that Ryan felt the Spirit telling him to keep meeting with the missionaries.

Not long after, the elders were transferred, and Sisters Johnson and Hardman replaced them. I continued to accompany them to lessons, along with other ward members. The answers we provided were not polished and perfect, but Ryan realized it was okay to ask questions, and we were willing to address his concerns. He later said, "I finally knew enough to push the rest of my intellectual concerns aside and respond to the Spirit I had been feeling for some time. I did not know everything, but what I learned was enough for me to trust God for everything I still desired to know."

Ryan asked to be baptized on Silvia's birthday. In the weeks leading up to the date, Ryan finished the Book of Mormon and the Pearl of Great Price, and he set a goal to dive into the Doctrine and Covenants next. He came to church and met with ward leaders and members for lessons and social gatherings. I was honored to be invited to perform the ordinance.

When we practiced, Ryan told me his full name: Ryan John Paul London. That's when it hit me how truly Catholic his family is. He was named after a pope! I said, "I know this is going to be hard for your parents to accept, but I hope one day they will understand."

Ryan responded, "I just have to keep Silvia and Benny in my mind right now."

On the special day, we showed up at the stake center and changed into white clothes. When Ryan and I entered the font, I knew that in a few moments, this once-in-a-lifetime experience would be over, and I wanted Ryan to have a bit more time to take it all in. Before baptizing him, I turned Ryan toward the group and told him to look at his wife and son. I pointed out the stake president, mission president, and missionaries. He also saw members of the bishopric and friends from the ward smiling down at him. "Ryan," I said, "don't ever forget how many people love and support you. You are not alone." Then I baptized Ryan John Paul into the Church of Jesus Christ. Considering the perspective that Pope John Paul now has, I am hopeful that he approved.

In the months that followed, Ryan and Silvia traveled to several temples to do baptisms for the dead. As the only members in both their families, there is plenty of work to do. Ryan continued to read the scriptures and books about Church doctrine. There were moments of discouragement along the way. Ryan's decision hurt his parents deeply, and learning to pay tithes and offerings was an adjustment. Nevertheless, Ryan and Silvia moved forward toward their goal of being sealed in the temple. When the next general conference came around, they wanted to attend one of the sessions in the Conference Center. As they walked across Temple Square, they reflected on how much their lives had changed since their first visit together there. During the session, Ryan was touched by the words of Elder Neil L. Andersen about the eternal truths found within the Family Proclamation, including the sanctity of life.[1] Ryan told me later, "I realized that policies and practices may change, but truth is eternal. As the Apostle spoke, I felt the Spirit swirling inside of me confirming the correctness of his words and my choice to join the Church."

The same Spirit that assured Ryan of the reality of God and the same Spirit that encouraged him to keep seeing the missionaries was now testifying that the sacrifices he was making are worth it. Who found Ryan? Was it the people in the Catholic church who nurtured his faith when he was young? Was it the people who made the TV documentary about the Church? Was it the friend who sent a Book of Mormon, or Silvia, who took him to a temple open house? Was it the first missionaries who attempted to teach him and wrote about him and his questions in their area record, or other missionaries who read the notes and tried once more? Was it members of the ward who befriended him, or was it me because I had the privilege of performing the baptism? We all played our parts, but it was God who knew where Ryan was hidden, found him, and generously allowed the rest of us to help.

President Thomas S. Monson once wrote, "No words in Christendom mean more to me than those spoken by the angel to the weeping Mary Magdalene and the other Mary as they approached the tomb to care for the body of their Lord: 'Why seek ye the living among the dead? He is not here, but is risen' (Luke 24:5–6). With this pronouncement, those who have lived and died, those who now live and one day will die, and those yet to be born and yet to die had just been rescued."[2]

Because of the Christ on Calvary, the lost can be found. All those who have lived, now live, and will one day live can be rescued, and we are commissioned to help. When I stood in the baptismal font and turned Ryan to see everyone who had helped him, I failed to acknowledge how much Ryan had helped all of us. The stake president, mission president, missionaries, family, and friends are all better off for having participated in this search-and-rescue mission. As we helped Ryan come closer to Christ, he helped us do the same. We lost ourselves and, as sure as scripture, found ourselves (see Matthew 10:39). God and Jesus care about the lost, but also about the seekers. Because of the Christ on Calvary, we can all be rescued.

SHALL THEIR UNBELIEF MAKE THE FAITH OF GOD WITHOUT EFFECT?

After Jesus miraculously fed thousands, many followed Him for the free food. He tried to lift their vision and expand their desires to higher levels: "And Jesus said unto them, I am the bread of life: he that cometh to me shall never hunger" (John 6:35). The people rejected the spiritual bread the Savior offered and "from that time many of his disciples went back, and walked no more with him" (v. 66). How heartbroken Christ must have felt as everyone abandoned Him except a few faithful: "Then said Jesus unto the twelve, Will ye also go away? Then Simon Peter answered him, Lord, to whom shall we go? thou hast the words of eternal life. And we believe and are sure that thou art that Christ, the Son of the living God" (vv. 67–69).

People at the Pew Research Center conducted phone interviews with 35,000 Americans from all fifty states to ascertain the religious landscape of America.[1] Results showed that many people—especially the younger generation—are leaving organized religion. Researchers asked, "Is religion very important?" Fifty-nine percent of my generation said yes, while only 41 percent of the younger generation said yes. There were marked differences in responses to other questions as well: "Do you attend weekly religious services?" (38% vs. 27%). "Do you pray at least once a day?" (61% vs. 42%). "Do you believe in heaven?" (74% vs. 67%).

The numbers are going down across the board. However, most Latter-day Saints do not need a research study to tell them that. We can all name friends and family members who once attended the Church of Jesus Christ but no longer participate. Some are going to other churches, but the vast majority are choosing to have no religious affiliation at all.[2] Some leave because of social issues, but that small group "receives a disproportionate amount of attention."[3] Most people leave because they have been hurt in some way, especially by divorce.[4] Those who are single and males who did not serve missions are also vulnerable.[5] Whatever the reason, this trend saddens me—not because we have fewer people in the Church, but because we have the Church in fewer people. Those who leave still deal with the struggles and challenges of life, but they are choosing to do it in the hardest way possible: without God, Christ, and the gospel.

Some people say they do not like organized religion.

Do the same people complain about organized airports? Most people would probably be quite upset if they tried to catch a flight in an airport where everyone believed and did whatever he or she felt like and no rules were established or enforced. To reject organized airports would be downright dangerous. Couldn't the same be said about rejecting organized religion?

One friend said, "I am okay with organized religion, but I don't like it when people say one church is better than any other because they are all the same." Are all countries the same? Are all hospitals, schools, and businesses? Whichever standards we choose to judge by, distinguishing between good and bad hospitals and schools seems to indicate that a person is intelligent and informed. Being able to select one business or product over another shows that a person is thoughtful and discerning. To embrace every church as equal is inaccurate.

Another friend said, "I'm a *spiritual* person. I am just not very *religious*." What she meant is that she is believing, kind, and ethical, but does not participate in formal church services. That is her right, but she is overlooking some important facts:

- Forty-five percent of people who attend religious services on a weekly basis report being very happy, as opposed to 28% of those who never attend.[6]

- People who attend religious services several times a week have the lowest reported number of mental health issues.[7]
- Religious people report having a greater sense of meaning in life[8] and cope better with illness and death.[9]
- Religious people donate to charity and volunteer for charitable causes much more than their secular counterparts.[10]

Elder Jeffrey R. Holland once spoke at Brigham Young University Education Week and explained that spirituality alone is insufficient. It might be fine if we all lived by ourselves on mountaintops, but we live in families, communities, and societies. That is why we need organized religion—the group practice of spirituality.[11]

Jesus did not live on a mountaintop. He sought times of solitude, but typically, He was in crowded villages mingling with the outcasts as well as the elite. He must have dealt with rebellious teens, out-of-control toddlers, and crying babies. He interacted with faithful followers and hateful attackers. Even among His closest disciples, there were different personalities. There were those who were loyal and dependable as well as those who doubted, denied, betrayed, and slept in His time of greatest need.

Similarly, today the gospel net gathers all kinds. We

have all sorts who face (and create) unique challenges. It would be easy to love if we were on a mountaintop with no one around who is unlovable. It is a little harder when we must minister to real people who struggle with real problems. It is easy to spout ideals about world peace and tolerance when we are alone, but try doing it in a traffic jam on the freeway. "Family first" are easy words to say in public but hard ones to live in private. Organized religion helps us combine mountaintop ideals with down-to-earth realities and gives us a place to practice the spirituality we preach.

People who do not want organized religion weighing them down are overrating the benefits of weightlessness. We have all seen recordings of astronauts floating around in space and think it looks fun. Perhaps it would be for a while, but scientists at NASA discovered early on in the space program that astronauts who spent too much time without restraints faced serious health consequences, including muscle atrophy and skeletal deterioration. That is why NASA officials later required astronauts to spend most of their time in space strapped down.[12]

Like astronauts who see the wisdom in restraint, Latter-day Saints realize we are better off because our organized religion comes with commandments, standards, and expectations. They keep us grounded, secure, safe, and happy. Elder Glenn L. Pace warned, "Don't mistake telestial pleasure for celestial happiness and joy. Don't mistake lack of self-control for freedom. Complete freedom without appropriate restraint makes us slaves to our appetites. Don't envy a lesser and lower life."[13] It is easy to understand why some people resist the cords and tethers that seem uncomfortable and binding, but we would not envy the astronaut who cuts the cord that connects him or her to the spacecraft and drifts aimlessly off into space. We would try to help that astronaut. When Church members cut their religious ties, we try desperately to revitalize the spiritual perspective and relationship with God that once made the rules and standards meaningful rather than burdensome.

Of course, no one is forced to stay in the Church. God will never demand our obedience but, as C. S. Lewis wrote, "There are only two kinds of people in the end: those who say to God, 'Thy will be done,' and those to whom God says, in the end, '*Thy* will be done.' All that are in Hell, choose it."[14] Even if, by some loophole, they were allowed into the celestial kingdom, taught Elder Neal A. Maxwell, "They would not be fully happy [there] anyway."[15]

In Romans 3:3 we read, "For what if some did not believe? shall their unbelief make the faith of God without effect?" Elder Jeffrey R. Holland responded, "No! Not in my life! Not in my lifetime! Not for me and my house! No one's unbelief has or can or will—ever—make my faith in God, my love of Christ, my devotion to this Church and this latter-day work 'without effect.'"[16]

People have rejected truth in every generation, and some have fought against truth in the past just as some do today. It does not change truth. Some call Latter-day Saints mindless sheep for following Christ and His prophets, but since when do mindless sheep go uphill? I saw a bumper sticker that said, "Religion—because thinking is hard." I do not know what religion the driver of that car was referring to, but I cannot name one thing about my faith, discipleship, and religion that could be described as easy. In Chile, Elder Holland repeated the following message in many stake conferences: "It's hard to be a member of the Church, but not nearly as hard as being out there without the Church."[17] Similarly, former Counselor in the Relief Society General Presidency Sheri Dew testified, "It's not living the gospel that's hard. It's *life* that's hard. . . . The gospel is the Good News that provides us the tools to cope with the mistakes, the heartaches, the disappointments we can expect to experience here."[18] With those words in mind, perhaps a more accurate bumper sticker would read: "Leaving religion— because growth is hard."

One student declared, "But I've studied the issues and discovered the Church is wrong." I responded, "How is it that I—and people who are a lot smarter than I am—have studied the same issues in much more depth and come to a different conclusion?" Sister Dew also wrote, "Doubters and pundits never tell the whole story, because they don't know the whole story and typically don't want to know. They opt for clever soundbites, hoping no one digs deeper than they have."[19] My fear is not that someone will find out something about the Church that causes moments of disequilibrium, but that he or she will not have the self-discipline required to study the issue in enough depth that surface knowledge can become understanding. My fear is that some people are making serious life decisions with no more information than what they see on social media. They see doubts as a reason to quit instead of a reason to learn more.

Another student asked, "How can I in good conscience stay in the Church when I see flaws?"

I replied, "Do you see flaws in your country? Do you know things about your country's history that do not sit well with you?"

"Of course."

I said, "Then where are your suitcases? Why aren't you leaving? How can you in good conscience stay in a country that has flaws?" Anyone can criticize or walk away; the more noble choice is to stay and strive to improve the status quo. We can be much more productive problem solvers working together on the inside than standing alone on the outside.

It is never easy to see someone choose to leave the Church. Some of the saddest and most painful moments of my life have been when I learn that some of my relatives, former missionaries, or former students have chosen to stop believing. In such low moments, I find comfort in what the Savior said to Judas: "[What] thou doest, do quickly" (John 13:27). It is sad that anyone would choose to leave and learn the hard way, but it seems some people refuse to learn any other way. They will find, as American writer Minna Thomas Antrim put it, "Experience is a good teacher, but she sends in terrific bills."[20] I cannot force people to stay, but I can pray they will return quickly and find the simplicity that awaits them on the other side of complexity.[21] I can hope that they will return to the testimonies they bore as children or new coverts and finally say the same words with greater depth and conviction. I can pray they internalize Christ's Atonement and discover His grace is sufficient and His promises are sure. I can recommit to staying on higher ground so I can lift them when they are ready.[22]

The fact that people are leaving religion does not change the fact that we need religion—especially *this* religion. Because of the Christ on Calvary, we do not have to face the challenges and hardships of life without Him and His restored gospel. Christ is the solution to every problem. Because Christ suffered and died on Calvary, He now stands on the highest ground. His arms are outstretched still (see 2 Nephi 19:12), ready to lift us up and hold us in His strong embrace (see Mormon 5:11).

COUNTING THE COST
AND MAKING IT COUNT

I met my wife Debi through her twin brother Doug. When I met him I was so impressed that I said, "You don't happen to have a twin sister I could marry, do you?"

"Actually, I do," Doug responded. "She is finishing her mission in Guatemala."

I met Debi a few weeks later when she spoke in sacrament meeting upon her return, and we were married about a year later.

The minute people discover Doug and Debi are twins, they always ask the same questions. Some are downright ridiculous, but people ask them anyway: Are you identical? (That is a curious one to ask a brother and sister.) Are you the same age? Can you read each other's minds? Do you ever look in the mirror and forget which one you are? Have you ever switched places? If I pinch you, will your twin feel it?

That last one is interesting because there are times when Doug and Debi feel each other's pain—not physically, but emotionally. I have witnessed that twin connection many times. When Doug went through some of the hardest times in his life, Debi went through them with him. Watching my wife suffer along with her brother gave me a better appreciation of Christ's Atonement.

Usually, Jesus's suffering tends to wash over us without sinking in. Even with all the hymns, talks, and artistic portrayals of Christ's passion, we do not always let it in. Maybe it is a good thing we do not feel His misery and grief all the time, or we would not be able to live our lives. However, now and then it is essential for us to bring down the protective wall we build around our hearts and truly contemplate Christ's suffering—to feel it as deeply as Debi felt the suffering of her twin brother Doug.

I will never forget being in Kaneohe, Hawaii, for a youth conference during which the teenagers participated in a special morning devotional called "Sensing Our Savior." They divided all the youth into groups of about eight or ten and took them to classrooms throughout the church building. I ended up in a group of young men and women that included some large, tough, Hawaiian football players. The leaders blindfolded us and began playing songs about the Savior's life and mission. Without saying a word, they placed objects in our hands—a handful of straw representing His birth, a piece of fishing net reminding us how He called His Apostles, and a washcloth reminiscent of the washing of the feet. With

Kenneth Cope's song "His Hands"[1] playing in the background, leaders placed spikes in our hands that we held as we listened. I had heard of similar sensory experiences, but I had never participated. It was moving to ponder the Savior's life and sacrifice in that way. It was also moving to see how respectful and reverent the youth were. I never expected those rough football players to be so somber and subdued. They let it in.

In Luke 14, the Lord taught about the cost of discipleship—that we are to forsake all and "bear his cross" (v. 27). He asked, "For which of you, intending to build a tower, sitteth not down first, and counteth the cost, whether he have sufficient to finish it?" (v. 28). I have always read those words thinking only of what He was asking us to do, but Christ never gave a commandment He did not keep. He gave up all. He bore His cross. He counted the cost and finished the Atonement so He could build not a tower, but us.

Now the question is whether we will choose to make His sacrifice count.

> *Christ never gave a commandment He did not keep.*

Elder Tad R. Callister taught, "As we expand our knowledge of the Atonement and increase our love for the Savior and the cause for which he suffered, our hearts begin to soften and more readily yield to the motivational powers of his sacrifice. We find new reservoirs of commitment to 'serve the living God.' Eventually, there emerges a personal burning resolve that his suffering shall not have been in vain."[2]

Evan is a young man who found that resolve. He grew up in California until he was ten. His family then moved to a small town in Idaho. They went to church, but church was not high on Evan's priority list. After high school graduation, Evan started thinking more about his future. He saw the light in people who were living the gospel and wanted it. They seemed positive, hopeful, and happy—everything he was not. He determined to start seeking what they had—next week. Then it got pushed off until next month and even next year. Looking back, Evan told me, "I wasn't just procrastinating moving upward, I was spiraling downward."

If people asked about a mission, Evan told them it was not for him. Then he turned twenty-one, and many of his friends who had chosen to serve were now home. "They were on fire about life and the Church," Evan said. "They were full of light." He was not on fire about anything. He had girlfriends and bad habits. The girlfriends never lasted. The bad habits did.

One night when Evan was especially low, he finally admitted to himself that what he was doing was not working. He wanted what his friends had and determined to go on a mission. He jumped through all the hoops, checked all the boxes, and was called to the Texas Houston South Mission.

Evan said, "I was not the best prepared missionary to ever enter the MTC, but I knew how to work and I desired to be obedient, so I figured that would count for something."

Evan discovered that the mission environment pushed regular emotions to extremes. Highs were higher and lows were lower. As he strove to be better and live closer to God, he became more aware of his flaws and weaknesses. He did not realize such feelings were normal and healthy.[3] He knew he had been forgiven and his slate had been wiped clean, but he did not yet see himself the way Heavenly Father saw him. He had not yet forgiven himself and released the pain associated with events that happened in his childhood or dealt with the resulting poor self-image. "You cannot hide from yourself in the mission," Evan said. "Things in my childhood had left a void which I had tried to fill in unhealthy ways. Suddenly those escapes were no longer an option. I had to face myself, and I did not like who I was." Evan had yet to learn that Christ's Atonement is for pain, depression, and low self-esteem as well as sins. It is about forgiving others who have hurt us as well as being forgiven ourselves. He had yet to learn that Christ is the only one who can truly fill all voids.

In the mission, Evan felt like a hypocrite. "If there is one thing I grew up disliking, it was hypocrisy, and now I looked the part of a missionary, but deep down I knew I had a past that needed to be dealt with. I had convinced myself that if people ever found out about my past, they would reject me. However, I finally got to the point that I did not care anymore. Everything I hid and suppressed for so many years needed to come out."

The Apostle Paul had a past too. He wrote, "I imprisoned and beat in every synagogue them that believed on [the Lord]: and when the blood of [the] martyr Stephen was shed, I also was standing by, and consenting unto his death, and kept the raiment of them that slew him" (Acts 22:19–20). Nevertheless, later, when Paul defended himself before Felix, he stated that he had a "conscience void of offence toward God, and toward men" (Acts 24:16). Some might ask, "How could someone guilty of so much have a clear conscience?" The answer is because of Jesus Christ. Paul knew it, and now Evan was learning it too.

Evan found out that hypocrisy is not slipping up as we are trying to change. That is discipleship. Hypocrisy is refusing to be honest with God, priesthood leaders, counselors, and ourselves. The minute Evan was honest with them, he no longer felt hypocritical. He felt free, clean, forgiven, and healed. Evan said, "I always assumed Christ's suffering was for others who were more deserving and worthy—the people who liked church. Now I realized that Christ did it for me, and I felt overwhelmed with gratitude." Evan let it in. It is not easy for our limited minds to comprehend Christ's limitless love, but every now and then our souls, like Enoch's, open "wide as eternity" (Moses 7:41), and we let it in.

As Evan counted the cost of Christ's sacrifice, it left him determined to make it count. He committed to be the best missionary ever—a high that lasted a few days before the realities of mission life pulled him back to earth. Having a testimony of Christ and His Atonement did not automatically make missionary work easy. Evan was learning that experiencing the miracle of forgiveness and healing did not mean other people lined up for baptism.

Missionaries study. That was hard for a young man who had never enjoyed school. Missionaries teach and testify—hard for a young man who had always avoided giving talks and testimonies. Evan started to wonder whether he was cut out for missionary work. He was grateful for how his mission had helped him personally, but he did not feel like he was doing much good for anyone else. The mental struggle of dealing with the past had been so exhausting, he wondered if it might be better for him to go home and continue the healing process there. Evan spoke with his mission president and parents about it and they said it was his choice. "Still," Evan said, "when I looked in the mirror, I did not see the light that I had seen in my friends when they returned home. I did not feel the fire they felt. I no longer saw a hypocrite, but I did not see the man I wanted to see. I decided I would give it one more day, and another after that, and another after that."

Then Evan met Harvey—not a new friend, but a hurricane. In 2017, Harvey tied with Hurricane Katrina as the most destructive tropical cyclone ever to hit the United States. Unprecedented rainfall caused severe flooding throughout the Houston metropolitan area and all over southeast Texas. Over one hundred people died, 17,000 needed rescue, and 30,000 were displaced from their homes. In all, the hurricane did 125 billion dollars' worth of damage. It affected Latter-day Saint chapels and the Houston Temple.

Evan and the other missionaries and volunteers sprang into action. They went from home to home ripping out carpet, tearing down walls, carrying out ruined furniture. Evan was in heaven. "I had done manual labor and construction my whole life, so I was in my element," he said. "We were working from the minute we woke up to the minute we went to bed." No longer did he wonder if he had anything to offer or if his skills and talents were needed. No longer did he question whether he had been sent to the right mission. He knew God had placed him there "for such a time as this" (Esther 4:14). Evan said, "What if I had gone home? What if I had been in Idaho when God needed me in Texas?" Even now, Evan marvels at seeing God's hand in his life so clearly.

"Harvey was a reset for me," said Evan. "I didn't have time to think about myself or focus on the past. I just worked and served others. I found out that living the gospel brings happiness. I am not talking about rainbows and pots of gold. I am just talking about feeling good about yourself—looking in the mirror and finally liking what you see." Evan would write in his journal, "I feel good. I feel happy." He purposely recorded those feelings so that if he ever doubted them down the road, he could look back and see proof.

Evan's mission president confirmed, "From Harvey on, you have never seen a better missionary. He was full of light and love for others. He was on fire." His mission president saw in him the very things that Evan had seen in his returned missionary friends. Evan said, "My mission was a miracle, but not like parting the Red Sea or changing water to wine. This miracle took a lot of time. The bands that held me down fell away, but it involved a lot of people and prayer over a long time. I felt the love of others and the love of the Lord and finally found a way to share it."

Counting the cost and making it count is not something we do alone. It is what Christ is doing with us. It is not just something that happens on missions, but throughout our lives. Since Evan's mission, he is working construction. He faces temptations and has to stay focused on moving forward along the covenant path. Evan says, "Now I am putting into practice everything I studied and taught on my mission. Christ's grace is there for me now just as it was before. It gets me through one day, and then another, and then another."

Because of the Christ on Calvary, Evan can look back at the child and teen he once was with compassion instead of hatred. Because of Christ, we, like

> *Counting the cost and making it count is not something we do alone. It is what Christ is doing with us.*

Evan, can experience miracles—the miracles of faith, repentance, forgiveness, and healing. We can find ways to use our talents and gifts to make a difference. Because of the Christ on Calvary, we can count the cost and—together with Him—make it count.

CONCLUSION

M any people in the world may not want God or religion, but they want a better life. At the beginning of this book I offered the invitation to consider what it is that you want most and then realize that God and religion—especially the restored gospel of Jesus Christ—can help you reach those goals.

Easter prompts us to stay focused on what really matters. It is an annual reminder that a better life and a better version of ourselves is within reach. On Easter, our family sings hymns at church, but we also sing a hymn at home that my mom, Val C. Wilcox, wrote with her good friend Janice Kapp Perry. It is called, "This Is He, This Is Jesus the Christ." I appreciate Sister Perry for giving me permission to include it in this book so you can sing along with us.

When I sing the lyrics, I hear my mother's testimony. She connected the dots. Her life was better because she knew that Christ was foreordained to come to earth to perform the

Atonement. She knew He came again to restore the fullness of His gospel, and she knew He will come again. She and my father shared their testimonies through the words they spoke and the choices they made. Their lives were full of peace and joy because of the gospel. Their divine center helped them live selflessly and purposefully. It was not always easy. They wrestled with the same struggles we all face. They were not blind to problems in the world, the Church, or our family, but they were bound to the Lord by covenants. They grew in their relationship with Him and trusted His grace. They never gave up seeking a better life for themselves and their children. They always looked to the Savior as "the right way, the saving truth, [and] the abundant life" [see John 14:6].[1] Even though they are gone now, their legacy of faith continues.

My life is better because they taught me about Easter's purposes, privileges, proofs, and promises. I hope they know that I value the Savior and His Grace and recognize the miracles of Christ's Atonement. I honor Christ's witnesses past and present and enjoy the blessings of worship and discipleship in my life.

Because of the Christ on Calvary, our past can be in the past. Our lives and futures can be better. Our efforts and offerings can matter. Our dreams can be fulfilled now and throughout eternity—all because of the King on the cross, the Christ on Calvary.

This Is He, This Is Jesus the Christ

Words by
Val Camenish Wilcox

Music by
Janice Kapp Perry

With conviction ♩ = 80

1. Mar-y bore God's own son, as a small help-less one. From the
2. Je-sus Christ, our dear Lord, and His gos-pel re-stored Of-fer
3. What a glo-ri-ous sight when he comes in his might From the

mo-ment of birth, the Mes-si-ah to earth. In a
ful-ness and light to each seek-er of right. Peace and
east, robed in red, as the proph-ets have said. He shall

time of great strife, thru His death He gave life. This is
com-fort they bring when His saints glad-ly sing This is
come in the day when the whole world will say, This is

He, this is Je-sus the Christ.
He, this is Je-sus the Christ.
He, this is Je-sus the Christ.

NOTES

INTRODUCTION

1. Dieter F. Uchtdorf, "The Gift of Grace," *Ensign*, May 2015, 107.

CHRIST AT THE CROSSROADS

1. See Marshall T. Burton, "Meridian of Time," in Daniel H. Ludlow, ed., *Encyclopedia of Mormonism* (New York: Macmillan, 1992), 2:891–92.

2. The Joseph Smith Papers, History, 1838–1856, volume E-1 [1 July 1843–30 April 1844]," p. 1974, accessed May 29, 2019, https://www.josephsmithpapers.org/paper-summary/history-1938-1856-volume-e-1-1-july-1843-30-april-1844/346.

3. "Our Identity and Our Destiny," Brigham Young University devotional address, 14 August 2012, 1. See speeches.byu.edu.

4. "The Origin of Man," *Improvement Era*, November 1909, 80.

5. "He Knows Who I Am," *New Era*, October 2012, 26.

6. "You Matter to Him," *Ensign*, November 2011, 20.

7. "Act II: Mortality," in *Joy in the Journey* (Salt Lake City: Deseret Book, 1998), 73.

8. Thanks to Teresa Edwards, who helped me think this concept through.

AN INFINITE AND ETERNAL SACRIFICE

1. In *Journal of Discourses*, 27 vols., ed. G. D. Watt. (London, England: Latter-day Saints' Book Depot, 1857), 10:175.

2. "The Atonement," *Ensign*, November 1996, 35.

3. *Articles of Faith* (Salt Lake City: The Church of Jesus Christ of Latter-day Saints, 1962), 78.

4. *Mere Christianity* (New York: Harper Collins, 1952), 50.

5. See Jeffrey R. Holland, "The Cost—and Blessings—of Discipleship," *Ensign*, May 2014, 6–9.

6. *When Heaven Feels Distant* (Salt Lake City: Deseret Book, 2018), 20; see also David A. Bednar, "If Ye Had Known Me," *Ensign*, November 2016, 102–5.

7. "One by One," Brigham Young University devotional address, 9 September 1997, 4. See speeches.byu.edu.

8. "A Pattern for All," *Ensign*, November 2005, 75–76.

9. See Fiona Givens and Terryl Givens, *The Christ Who Heals: How God Restored the Truth That Saves Us* (Salt Lake City: Deseret Book, 2017), 45.

THE HOLY WEEK AND THE HOLY CROSS

1. See Wendee Wilcox Rosborough, *The Holy Week for Latter-day Saint Families: A Guide for Celebrating Easter* (Salt Lake City: Deseret Book, 2016).

2. "The Symbol of Our Faith," *Ensign*, April 2005, 3.

3. *The Christ Who Heals: How God Restored the Truth That Saves Us* (Salt Lake City: Deseret Book, 2017), 110.

4. *What Happened to the Cross? Distinctive LDS Teachings* (Salt Lake City: Deseret Book, 2007), 104; italics in original.

5. See John Hilton III, "Teaching the Scriptural Emphasis on the Crucifixion," *The Religious Educator*, vol. 20, no. 3, 133–53; "The Use of 'Gethsemane' by Church Leaders: 1859–2018," *BYU Studies Quarterly*, in press.

6. "The Atonement of Jesus Christ," *Ensign*, May 2019, 85.

7. "The Correct Name of the Church," *Ensign*, November 2018, 88; italics in original.

FIVE SCRIPTURES I USED TO DISLIKE, BUT NOW I LOVE

1. Fiona Givens and Terryl Givens, *The Christ Who Heals: How God Restored the Truth That Saves Us* (Salt Lake City: Deseret Book, 2017), 53.

2. *The Christ Who Heals*, 58.

3. See Terryl L. Givens, *By the Hand of Mormon* (New York: Oxford University Press, 2003), 206–7.

4. "Willing to Submit," *Ensign*, May 1985, 72–73.

5. "My Testimony," *Ensign*, May 2000, 71.

6. *Lighten Up!* (Salt Lake City: Deseret Book, 1993), 176.

7. Robert D. Hales, "Behold, We Count Them Happy Which Endure," *Ensign*, May 1998, 75.

8. Jeffrey R. Holland, "None Were with Him," *Ensign*, May 2009, 88.

9. See Shon Hopkin, "'My God, My God, Why Hast Thou Forsaken Me?' Psalm 22 and the Mission of Christ," *BYU Studies Quarterly*, 52, no. 4, 2013, 117.

10. "'My God, My God, Why Hast Thou Forsaken Me?,'" 142.

11. "'My God, My God, Why Hast Thou Forsaken Me?,'" 142.

A TALE OF TWO TOMBS

1. "Preparing for the Lord's Return," *Ensign*, May 2019, 81.

2. A survey shows that a large portion of Christians polled do not believe Jesus actually rose from the dead in a physical form. See "Resurrection did not happen, say quarter of Christians," BBC News: available at http://www.bbc.com/news/uk-england-39153121.

3. *Eternal Man* (Salt Lake City: Deseret Book, 1970), 44–51.

4. I appreciate my brother, Roger Wilcox, for explaining Doctrine and Covenants 76 so clearly.

5. See *Saints: The Standard of Truth* (Salt Lake City: The Church of Jesus Christ of Latter-day Saints, 2018), 1:146–50.

6. See *Saints*, 1:421–22.

7. Later, President Joseph F. Smith clarified, "There is a time after this mortal life, and there is a way provided by which we may fulfil the measure of our . . . destiny." Funeral Sermon preached 11 April 1878, in *Journal of Discourses*, 26 vols., reported by G. D. Watt et al. Liverpool: F. D. and S. W. Richards, et. al., 1851–1856, 19:264. In Alma 34:33 we learn after "this life" will come "the night of darkness wherein there can be no labor performed." Since temple work can be done for those in the spirit world, "this life" can include the spirit world.

8. The Joseph Smith Papers, History, 1838–1856, volume D-1 [August 1842–1 July 1843] [addenda]," p. 4 [addenda], https://www.josephsmithpapers.org/paper-summary/history-1838-1856-volume-d-1-1-august-1842-1-july-1843/285.

9. *Saints*, 1:523.

10. *Saints*, 1:523.

11. The Joseph Smith Papers: "Discourse, 3 October 1841, as reported by Times and Seasons," 577. Retrieved from https://www.josephsmithpapers.org/paper-summary/discourse-3-october-1841-as-reported-by-times-and-seasons/1; italics in original.

12. *Saints*, 1:524–28.

13. Notes from a presentation by Robert J. Matthews in a CES Summer Inservice in Orem, Utah, 10 July 1986, as quoted in Todd Parker, *Rel A 121: Notes, Quotes, Handouts, and Study Questions—Book of Mormon 1st Half* (Provo, UT: Brigham Young University), 142.

14. See John Hilton III and Anthony Sweat, *The Big Picture* (Salt Lake City: Deseret Book, 2012), 198.

15. Dallin H. Oaks, "Trust in the Lord," *Ensign*, November 2019, 29.

16. Funeral Sermon preached April 11, 1878, in *Journal of Discourses*, 26 vols., reported by G. D. Watt, et al. (Liverpool: F. D. and S. W. Richards, et. al., 1851–1856), 19:264.

17. Fiona Givens and Terryl Givens, *The Christ Who Heals: How God Restored the Truth That Saves Us* (Salt Lake City: Deseret Book, 2017), 121.

18. *Articles of Faith* (Salt Lake City: The Church of Jesus Christ of Latter-day Saints, 1962), 114.

19. "The Paths Jesus Walked," *Ensign*, May 1974, 49.

20. Brigham Young, in *Journal of Discourses*, 26 vols. (London: Latter-day Saints' Book Depot, 1854–1886), 4:268.

REPENTANCE: CLEAR AS CRYSTAL

1. Thanks to Philip Enkey for this insight.

2. Thanks to Cap Cresap for pointing this verse out to me.

3. See Clifford P. Jones, "The Great and Marvelous Change: An Alternative Interpretation," *Journal of the Book of Mormon Studies*, vol. 19, no. 2 (Provo, UT: The Neal A. Maxwell Institute for Religious Scholarship, 2010), 50–63.

4. Thanks to Jen Spencer for this analogy.

5. Bruce C. Hafen and Marie K. Hafen, *The Belonging Heart: The Atonement and Relationships with God and Family* (Salt Lake City: Deseret Book, 1994), 79; italics in original.

6. See https://www.biblestudytools.com/lexicons/greek/nas/teleios.html.

7. "Can You Hear the Music?" Brigham Young University devotional address, 15 January 2019, 7–8. See speeches.byu.edu.

TO RUN TO OUR AID

1. Jennifer Reeder and Janiece Johnson, *The Witness of Women: Firsthand Experiences and Testimonies from the Restoration* (Salt Lake City: Deseret Book, 2016).

2. Jennifer Reeder and Kate Holbrook, *At the Pulpit: 185 Years of Discourses by Latter-day Saint Women* (Salt Lake City: Church Historians Press, 2017).

3. *The Atoning One* (Salt Lake City: Deseret Book, 2018), 60; italics in original.

4. "Bear Up Their Burdens with Ease," *Ensign*, May 2014, 90.

5. Thanks to Jackson Ockey for the German translation; see also Fiona Givens and Terryl Givens, *The Christ Who Heals: How God Restored the Truth That Saves Us* (Salt Lake City: Deseret Book, 2017), 64.

6. See Daniel K. Judd, W. Justin Dyer, and Justin B. Top, "Grace, Legalism, and Mental Health: Examining Direct and Mediating Relationships," *Psychology of Religion and Spirituality*; advance online publication, http://dx.doi.org/10.1037; re10000211.

7. See https://www.merriam-webster.com/dictionary/succor.

OUR GOD WITH US JOINING

1. See S. Michael Wilcox, *Ten Great Souls I Want to Meet in Heaven* (Salt Lake City: Deseret Book, 2012), 15–31.

2. See https://www.merriam-webster.com/dictionary/redeem.

3. "Born of God," *Ensign*, November 1985, 6.

4. "The Gift of Grace," *Ensign*, May 2015, 107.

5. See D. Todd Christofferson, "The Power of Covenants," *Ensign*, May 2009, 22.

6. *The Problem of Pain* (New York: Harper Collins, 1940), 35.

7. "The Paths Jesus Walked," *Ensign*, September 1992, 4.

8. D. Todd Christofferson, "Free Forever, to Act for Themselves," *Ensign*, November 2014, 19.

9. Thanks to Philip Enkey for this insight.

THE ROLE OF FAITH

1. "Is Yours a Believing Heart?" *Ensign*, September 1974, 55.

2. See Terryl and Fiona Givens, *The God Who Weeps* (Salt Lake City: Ensign Peak, 2012), 4–5.

3. "Can You Hear the Music?" Brigham Young University devotional address, 15 January 2019, 5. See speeches.byu.edu.

4. See Lawrence Corbridge, "Stand Forever." Brigham Young University devotional address, 22 January, 2019, 4. See speeches.byu.edu.

5. See James S. Jacobs and Michael O. Tunnell, *Children's Literature, Briefly* (Upper Saddle River, NJ: Merrill Prentice Hall, 1996), 72–73.

6. "Can You Hear the Music?," 4.

ANOTHER TESTAMENT

1. See *World Christian Encyclopedia* (Oxford University Press, 2nd edition, 2001); see also http://www.philvaz.com/apologetics/a106.htm.

2. Robert I. Heaton and Henry J. Eyring, *I Will Lead You Along: The Life of Henry B. Eyring* (Salt Lake City: Deseret Book, 2013), 30.

MODERN PROPHETS' WITNESSES OF CHRIST

1. See https://www.churchofjesuschrist.org/church/news/joseph-smith-atop-smithsonian-magazines-top-religious-figures-list?lang=eng.

2. *Saints*, 1:542–43.

3. I attended a stake conference in Sacramento, California, on 24 February 2019, where Elder Jeffrey R. Holland testified of this truth using these words.

4. *We're with You: Counsel and Encouragement from Your Brethren* (Salt Lake City: Deseret Book, 2016).

INFALLIBLE PROOFS

1. See Andrew C. Skinner, *The Garden Tomb* (Salt Lake City: Deseret Book, 2005), 185; see also *Strong's Concordance*, biblehub.com/greek/1404.htm.

2. See *Doctrinal New Testament Commentary*, Vol. 2. (Salt Lake City: Bookcraft, 1971), 22.

3. Thanks to Steve Smoot, who helped me clarify the distinctions between these three titles.

4. See *The Crown Jewels* (Surrey, UK: Historic Royal Palaces, 2018).

5. *The Crown Jewels*, 11.

6. *The Crown Jewels*, 21.

7. See *The Crown Jewels*, 38.

8. *The Gospel Kingdom, Collector's Edition* (Salt Lake City: Bookcraft, 1987), 229.

DISAPPOINTED WITH GOD

1. See Philip Yancey, *Disappointment with God: Three Questions No One Asks Aloud* (Grand Rapids, MI: Zondervan Publishing, 1988).

2. *Disappointment with God*, 26.

3. *Disappointment with God*, 35.

4. *Disappointment with God*, 36.

5. *Disappointment with God*, 44; italics in original.

6. See Richard Neitzel Holzapfel, Eric D. Huntsman, and Thomas A. Wayment, *Jesus Christ and the World of the New Testament* (Salt Lake City: Deseret Book, 2006), 186.

7. *One to One: Understanding Personal Relationships* (New York: Forge, 1983), 219.

8. "Lest Ye Be Weary and Faint in Your Minds," *Ensign*, May 1991, 88.

9. "This Do in Remembrance of Me," *Ensign*, November 1995, 69; italics in original.

10. See Marion D. Hanks, "A Loving, Communicating God," *Ensign*, November 1992, 64.

11. "'Fear Not, I Am with Thee': The Redeeming, Strengthening, and Perfecting Blessings of Christ's Atonement," *Religious Educator*, vol. 16, no. 1, 24.

12. *Disappointment with God*, 45; italics in original.

13. See Michael Gradisar, Kate Jackson, Nicola J. Spurrier, Joyce Gibson, Justine Whitham, Anne Sved Williams, Robyn Dolby, and David J. Kennaway, "Behavioral Interventions for Infant Sleep Problems: A Randomized Controlled Trial," *Pediatrics*, vol. 137, no. 6, 2016, 1–10. I appreciate Sara Pulsipher for bringing this study to my attention when she presented at the 21st Annual Religious Education Student Symposium, 15 February 2019, Brigham Young University.

14. See Karen E. Adolph, Whitney G. Cole, Meghana Komati, Jessie S. Garciaguirre, Daryaneh Badaly, Jesse M. Lingeman, Gladys L. Y. Chan, and Rachel B. Sotsky, "How Do You Learn to Walk? Thousands of Steps and Dozens of Falls per Day," *Psychological Sciences*, vol. 23, no. 11, 2012, 1387–94. I appreciate Sara Pulsipher for bringing this study to my attention.

15. "Learning to Recognize Answers to Prayer," *Ensign*, November 1989, 31.

16. *Disappointment with God*, 46; italics in original.

17. A more complete discussion of this topic can be found in a book I wrote with John Hilton III, *52 Life-Changing Questions from the Book of Mormon* (Salt Lake City: Deseret Book, 2013), 155–59.

18. Lucile C. Tate, *Boyd K. Packer: A Watchman on the Tower* (Salt Lake City: Bookcraft, 1995), 60.

SEARCH AND RESCUE

1. See "The Eye of Faith," *Ensign*, May 2019, 36.

2. "He Is Not Here, but Is Risen," *Ensign*, April 2011, 4.

SHALL THEIR BELIEF MAKE
THE FAITH OF GOD WITHOUT EFFECT?

1. See https://www.pewforum.org/about-the-religious-landscape-study/.

2. See Stephen Cranney, "Who Is Leaving the Church?: Demographic Predictors of Ex-Latter-day Saint Status in the Pew Religious Landscape Study," *BYU Studies Quarterly*, Vol. 58, no. 1 (2019), 99–108; see also "The Rise of 'no religion,'" Analysis of General Social survey data by Ryan Burge, *Deseret News*, 21 April 2019, P-4.

3. "Who Is Leaving the Church?," 107.

4. "Who Is Leaving the Church?," 106.

5. See Jana Riess, *The Next Mormons: How Millennials Are Changing the LDS Church* (New York: Oxford University Press, 2019).

6. See http://www.breitbart.com/national-security/2014/12/24/religious-people-much-happier-than-others-new-study-shows/; see also Jeff Levin, "Religious Behavior, Health, and Well-Being among Israeli Jews: Findings from the European Social Survey," *Psychology of Religion and Spirituality*, vol. 5, no. 4 (November 2013), 272–82.

7. See http://www.baylor.edu/content/services/document.php/153501.pdf.

8. See http://onlinelibrary.wiley.com/doi/10.1111/jssr.12170/abstract.

9. See Christina M. Puchalski, "The Role of Spirituality in Health Care," *Baylor University Medical Center Proceedings*, 14 (4), 353.

10. See Arthur C. Brooks, "Religious Faith and Charitable

Giving," *Policy Review*, Issue 121 (October–December 2003), 39–50; see also "Faith Matters Survey 2006," as cited by Robert A. Putnam and David E. Campbell in *American Grace: How Religion Divides and Unites Us* (New York: Simon and Schuster, 2010).

11. See "Religion: Bound by Loving Ties," Brigham Young University devotional address, 16 August 2016, 2. See speeches .byu.edu.

12. I appreciate Daren Saunders, who has taught many young people about the dangers of spiritual weightlessness.

13. "They're Not Really Happy," *New Era*, June 1988, 5.

14. *The Great Divorce* (New York City: Harper Collins, 1946), 75; italics in original.

15. *One More Strain of Praise* (Salt Lake City: Bookcraft, 1999), 39.

16. "Be Not Afraid, Only Believe," address to CES Religious Educators, 6 February 2015, Salt Lake Tabernacle, 3–4.

17. Personal communications, 2003–4.

18. "We Are Not Alone," *Ensign*, November 1998, 94.

19. *Worth the Wrestle* (Salt Lake City: Deseret Book, 2017), 24.

20. *Naked Truth and Veiled Allusions* (Philadelphia, PA: Henry Altenios, 1901), 99.

21. See Bruce C. Hafen and Marie K. Hafen, *Faith Is Not Blind* (Salt Lake City: Deseret Book, 2018), 7–18.

22. See Harold B. Lee, "Stand Ye in Holy Places," *Ensign*, July 1973, 123.

COUNTING THE COST AND MAKING IT COUNT

1. *Greater Than Us All* (Salt Lake City: Embryo Music, 1989).

2. *The Infinite Atonement* (Salt Lake City: Deseret Book, 2000), 217–18.

3. "The closer we come to the City of God, the more we will notice the remaining distance and our remaining weaknesses.

. . . The best people have a heightened awareness of what little of the worst is still in them!" (Neal A. Maxwell, *Notwithstanding My Weakness* [Salt Lake City: Deseret Book, 1981], 16–17.)

CONCLUSION

1. Ezra Taft Benson, "Born of God," *Ensign*, November 1985, 5.

ABOUT THE AUTHOR

Brad Wilcox is an associate professor in the Department of Ancient Scripture at Brigham Young University, where he also enjoys teaching at Campus Education Week and Women's Conference. He speaks at Time Out for Women events and is the author of *The Continuous Atonement*, *The Continuous Conversion*, *The 7-Day Christian*, and the BYU devotional "His Grace Is Sufficient." In 2018, his book *Because of the Messiah in a Manger* topped the best-seller list. This book is a companion to that volume. As a young man, Brad served his mission in Chile, and in 2003 he returned to that country to preside over the Chile Santiago East Mission for three years. He also served as a member of the Sunday School general board from 2009 to 2014. Brad and his wife, Debi, have four children and eight grandchildren.